UNTAPPED

Break through the fear & grow your revenue from existing clients

JAMES ASHFORD

Author of the No.1 bestseller

SELLING TO SERVE

UNTAPPED by JAMES ASHFORD

3 5 7 9 10 8 6 4 2

First Published 2022

Edited by Charlie Rasbuary & The GoProposal Community

Acknowledgements

Every effort has been made to trace copyright holders. The publishers will be glad to rectify in future editions any errors or omissions brought to their attention.

Published by GoProposal Limited. Registered in England with Company Registration No: 10004041. Registered Office: C23 - 5 & 6 Cobalt Park Way Cobalt Park, Newcastle Upon Tyne, United Kingdom, NE28 9EJ

For more information visit www.GoProposal.com

Untapped

[ənˈtæpt] *noun*

not being used yet, but existing in large amounts that could bring profits or benefits.

Contents

TWO LUMBERJACKS

Before we start, I want to tell you a well-known story of two lumberjacks.

Every day, they start at the same time and finish at the same time.

One of them works non-stop throughout the day, chopping wood.

But the other one, keeps stopping throughout the day and disappearing.

Every day, the one who keeps disappearing has chopped more wood than the other.

This goes on for months.

Eventually, the guy who works flat-out all day, turns to the one who keeps disappearing and says, "I don't get it. I work **non-stop** all day and you keep disappearing. Yet every day you have more wood than me. Where do you go when you disappear?"

"Oh," said the other lumberjack. "That's easy. I go and sharpen my axe."

Devoting time to reading this book and actioning what you learn, is time out to sharpen your axe.

You do this whenever you take time out of your busy day to read a book, watch a useful video, do a course, take mentoring or work *on* your business, not *in* it.

The best use of your time is spent sharpening your axe.

INTRODUCTION

There are two lenses through which people tend view the world: one of **scarcity** and one of **abundance.**

Depending on which one you look through, will determine what you see and what you believe is possible for you to achieve.

You could literally be sat on an absolute diamond mine with a scarcity mindset and see nothing but rocks.

Or you could be sat on a pile of rocks, but have an abundance mindset, see nothing but diamonds.

In May 2021, an accountant posted in the GoProposal Facebook Community (I'm the founder of GoProposal in case you didn't know.)

He explained how his clients were unwilling to pay more money, which in turn, made him question his own costs. As a result, he was contemplating downgrading his GoProposal subscription so he could save £60 a month, even though it meant he'd be limiting the number of proposals he could produce each month and other members of his team wouldn't be able to use it.

This was slap-bang in the middle of the global pandemic, where businesses and economies had been decimated, where the news was a barrage of negativity about death and loss and where it was very easy to slip into scarcity thinking.

I challenged his question and specifically, why he was so concerned over saving such a small amount, whereas if he just saw the cost as an *investment* and what it enabled, he could make that back tenfold, in a very short space of time.

Why devote so much brain power to such a small saving I thought, rather than engaging the brain to explore ways to generate great wealth and ways to deliver so much more value?

The conversation went backwards and forwards, but with little progress.

I became frustrated.

I delivered my usual rhetoric about how accounting and bookkeeping services are vital to the success of your clients' businesses. I talked about how, despite the pandemic, there is still so much money out there, about how all your clients' entire families have iPhones, large TVs on the wall, fancy cars on the drive and extravagant holidays booked. People don't have an issue getting what they want, in fact, they're prepared to go into debt for it.

Jeff Bezos knows this. Throughout the pandemic, Amazon sales rose to $1.4bn… a day. Jeff has no issue diverting some of their cash towards him, so why do you?

Why is it so difficult for you to see the incredible value you bring and to confidently charge more for it, especially when we've just been through such a historic event as the global pandemic, where the value of accountants and bookkeepers has gone THROUGH THE ROOF?

If your clients didn't know the value of your services before this happened, they certainly do now.

For years you've been preaching about how they needed a budget and a forecast so they know where they're heading, why they need management accounts so they know if they're on track and why they need you to run their payroll and bookkeeping accurately, so they can focus on driving their business forward, armed with the information you provide.

But few businesses saw the value. And to keep you accountable, you probably didn't show them or insist they took it.

For years, so many businesses have massively underinvested in their finance function and individuals have not seen the benefits of preparing accurate tax returns early enough, so they can consider minimising their tax liability or setting it to one side.

I'll say it again, if your clients didn't see the full value of what you do before the pandemic, they certainly do now.

Yet despite this, I'm still seeing firms scared to increase fees, whilst their clients are spending more on home TV packages than they are on their accounting bill.

This is how we get to a point where a very competent and brilliant accountant is obsessing over a £60 saving in their software costs, versus thinking… 'How can we make an extra £10k a month in fees this year?'

Then it hit me.

I realized what was missing.

All of the logic and facts I presented wasn't making a difference to this person, because I was seeing the world through my lens, and he was seeing it through his.

You see, as Anaïs Nin wrote, "We do not see things *as* they are, we see things as *we* are."

The default lens through which I view the world is one of **abundance**.

I believe that there is more than enough of everything you want out there, you just have to develop the mindset and the skills to tap into it.

This accountant was looking at the world the through the lens of **scarcity**.

Scarcity says the opposite, which is that there isn't enough of the things I'm looking for and as more people find them, there is less for me.

It doesn't matter what anyone says to you, it is the lens through which you perceive the world that will determine your response. I realised I hadn't done enough to help people develop an **abundant mindset.**

So, I announced that I would take 50 firms and over the course of 30 days, I would negate any £60 software costs they were concerned about, by helping them to generate significantly more than that in profit per month, from EXISTING CLIENTS, largely for the work they WERE ALREADY DOING.

And I vowed that it wouldn't involve any weird sales techniques or voodoo magic or anything they would feel uncomfortable with, just mathematically backed logic, a straightforward strategy and a reframing of their mindset.

Over the next 30 days, I helped those 50 firms to grow their collective annual revenue by over HALF A MILLION POUNDS. That equated to a little over £800 of monthly recurring revenue per firm… from existing clients... for the same work... and in some cases, even doing LESS work.

These weren't large firms, quite the opposite. These were mainly small and new firms, many of them were armies of one. So, you can imagine the impact this increase in revenue had on them.

And this process wasn't so much about what they achieved, but who they became by getting there. Just imagine if they continued that process with this renewed attitude, month on month, for 12 months with all their clients; what a very different leader they would be and firm they would have.

More and more firms heard about what we did and asked if they could be taken through the same process, and so I took another 50 firms and repeated the exercise two months later.

More than anything, I wanted to prove to myself that it wasn't a fluke the first time and that there wasn't some unusual quirk about the firms that engaged.

It happened again; 50 firms, 30 days, over half a million pounds in the growth of their collective annual recurring revenue.

This wasn't a fluke.

This was, in fact, the combination of over a decade's worth of work, of studying how to help businesses to get everything they can out of everything they've got, using proven, world-leading, growth strategies, combined with an unstoppable mindset. A decade of implementing those strategies and changing those mindsets to create immediate breakthroughs across thousands of accounting and bookkeeping businesses.

Word spread further and with the increasing uncertainty I was seeing in the world, I vowed to reach as many accounting businesses as I could, committing to laying out the exact process I took those 100 firms on, step by step in a book. *This* book.

And I'm not really sure what 'this' book is.

It isn't a conventional step-by-step guide, because while that's what you might think you want, they don't work. Unless you understand *why* you need to take the steps, why you need to take them *now*, what will happen if you *don't* and what will cause you to *stop or retreat from the process completely*, nothing changes.

Because if you don't approach it in that way, you won't get any real change, and if you do, it won't last.

Lasting change requires something quite different.

It requires us to take a deep journey within and to question why we do what we do, and why we're not further ahead than we'd like to be.

Because if you want to change the results you're getting in your life, in terms of more money, more time, more energy, more headspace and more happiness, then you have to fundamentally change your thinking.

The thinking that has gotten you to where you are, is not going to get you to where you need to be.

In order to do that, you must accept that part of your thinking, your beliefs and your behaviours, are in fact wrong.

But the truth is, most people don't want to change; they don't want to accept that they're wrong in any way.

They would much rather believe that they're right… than be happy.

This book isn't about giving you anything new necessarily; it's about stripping back and revealing to you what's been there all along.

It's about uncoupling you from thought patterns and beliefs which you've adopted over the years without even knowing where they came from.

You see, **you are already sitting on a diamond mine of clients.**

Clients who would willingly pay you so much more for the service you're already providing them.

Clients who, if asked correctly, would want much more from you… ten times more in some cases.

Clients who could be absolute diamonds for you, who are responsive to your requests, respectful of you and your team and who would massively value all the hard work you're doing for them.

So why aren't you seeing these untapped diamonds?

Why aren't they shining and twinkling and leaping out at you, for you just to grab if it's that easy?

Why do you believe that the diamonds you're *actually* looking for are somewhere out there, far away from the clients you currently have who, in your opinion, are nothing like diamonds… just rocks… holding you back, weighing you down and preventing you from getting to where you *really* want to get to?

Most people don't want to change; they don't want to accept that they're wrong in any way.

They would much rather believe that they're right... than be happy.

And even if there was some ounce of truth in what I was saying, and you *were* sitting on diamonds, there'd have to be a catch right? Like I'd expect you to have to learn some awful, manipulative sales technique that would make you feel so uncomfortable, you'd never actually use it; something that would sound convincing on the pages of a book, but that would have no practical bearing on the day-to-day running of a modern accounting business, operating in a post-covid world where everyone's watching their pennies and on their guard.

What I'm about to share with you is totally logical, very fair, will soon feel very comfortable for you and asks you to be no one other than you… your beautiful, wonderful self, who is more than good enough at what you do and who deserves greater rewards as a result, whatever they may be for you.

In fact, the strategy for achieving this is very straightforward.

So, if this really is as straightforward as I would have you believe, why aren't more firms doing it? Why are most firms still struggling, continuing to do more than they're getting paid for and despite that, still failing to carry out fee reviews with their clients, in some cases, for years?

Why, if this is such common sense, is it not common practice?

Well, I put this down to three main reasons…

1. You're afraid of one specific question
2. The fear is hard wired into you
3. Diamonds don't look like diamonds

THE ONE SPECIFIC QUESTION

There is one question you're afraid your clients will ask… "Why have my fees gone up?" or even worse, "Why have YOU put my fees up?"

And I don't mean being afraid of the question when you've simply raised your fees in line with inflation or because they have an extra member of staff or two on payroll.

I mean being afraid of that question when there is a **significant** increase in their fees, for what they perceive to be no additional work being done and when they've been used to paying much less for perhaps a long period of time.

And this normally occurs at the moment you realise you've been pricing way too low, for way too long and it will no longer support the growth of your firm.

I want you to imagine that moment; really picture it… you're sat there, face to face with that PITA client (Pain in The Ass), who you've had for years (you're picturing them right?) and you haven't increased their fees since forever. Your workload has been constantly increasing for them, their business has been growing, they're always on the phone and everyone dreads it when they ring.

BUT… and here's the rub... they pay a chunky fee. Nowhere near what they *should* be paying… but not one you want to lose.

And let's compound the problem by saying they're quite vocal, well known in the local area and very active on social media. You may even have some personal connection to them such as their kids are in the same school as yours, they go to the same gym as you or your dads play golf together… something really awkward like that.

So, you're sat in front of THAT client and deep down you know that you need to triple their fee, just for you to provide the same level of service they're getting now.

NOW would you be afraid of the question, "Why have my fees gone up?"

Because these are the types of conversations you may well need to have.

And when you have them, you need to be calm and professional AND at the end of the conversation, they need to willingly and happily accept the fee increase.

Throughout this book, not only will you galvanise your mindset to be able to deal with this strained scenario, but you will learn the set-responses, so it becomes second-nature to you and your team.

By the end of this book, you WILL be in a position to double, triple and even 10x fees and over time, it will become as natural as filing a tax return.

As far off as this may seem, so was completing a tax return once upon a time. This is just another skill to learn.

THE FEAR

While I will help you to strengthen your mindset, and I will give you the blueprint for all the possible ways the conversation may go, you will still feel *fear*.

This is perfectly natural and in fact, unavoidable.

It is hardwired into the oldest and most primitive part of your brain that's been evolving for hundreds of thousands of years – the reptilian part of your brain.

You see, your brain's function is **not** to help you to be hugely successful and get you everything you ever wanted in life.

It's not designed to help you to buy that sports car, live in that dream house, go on wonderful holidays with your family or to give you that six pack.

Your brain's function is to **keep you alive.**

It's designed to keep you with your tribe, by the fire, under a shelter, sharing the food and to prevent you from being eaten by a sabre tooth tiger.

If you hear a rustling in the bushes, your brain will tell you it's something that could eat you and will set you on high alert so you can deal with the possible threat.

What it won't do, is tell you to ignore it, and that it will be fine.

Your brain has learned over the millennia, that it's safer to warn you about a potential danger, even if it turns out *not* to be one, than to ignore it and for you to get eaten alive.

That's your brain's job. It has chemicals it can release, images it can conjure and voices that will chatter away to you incessantly, in order to help you avoid perceived dangers and possible threats.

If you were to consider the prospect of sitting in front of a client and increasing their fees, you know that there's a chance they could leave.

So, your brain tries to protect you by sparking a series of thoughts that go something like this…

What will happen if I increase their fees?

What will they say?

Will they leave?

How will we survive if I lose their income?

What if we can't replace that income?

What if they tell everyone I'm trying to rip them off?

What if people think I'm greedy and hate me?

What if other clients leave too?

In fact, what if all my clients leave?

How would I pay the bills?

How would I feed my family?

If I lost the business, would we have to downsize the house?

What if we have to sell the car?

How will that look to our family and friends?

Would we have to move in with the in-laws?

Will I have to get another job? Who'd employ me?

Screw it… let's keep that client's fee as it is, and I'll work even later.

I'll just find a better client instead.

Can you see how your brain works? It's just trying to keep you alive by protecting you from things it believes threatens your life, and your livelihood is very closely connected to that.

I'm going to share every strategy I know to rewire large parts of the brain, to counter those thought patterns and help you achieve massive success. But at the core of your brain is something called your **amygdala** and it has too many tricks up its sleeve for me or you to contend with.

It is capable of releasing stress hormones like cortisol and adrenaline which alerts your entire nervous system and sets your body's fear response into motion.

This can be so powerful and debilitating, as it treats the prospect of losing a client in the same way as if you were being physically attacked.

So how on earth can you turn that off?

In short… you can't.

I will not be able to remove the fear for you.

I can certainly minimise it and give you a logical thought process and battleplan to triumph over it, but if you're waiting for fear to disappear before you take any action, you will never move forward.

If you're waiting for fear to disappear before you take any action, you will never move forward.

We have to learn to move forward WITH fear and develop the confidence to know that it will be alright… and it will. In fact, it will be more than alright. And the more you do it, the more alright it will be and the quieter the voice of fear and associated feelings will become.

You will discover the mindset and blueprint that will unlock riches that are sat right under your nose, which you can't even see yet.

I just need to help you to reduce the fear to a point where you *can* see more clearly… and where you feel confident to take the actions that will get you what you deserve.

BUT… there is another reason you can't see the diamonds yet, even if you were brave enough to lift your head above the parapet to look.

And that's because, diamonds don't look like diamonds.

DIAMONDS DON'T LOOK LIKE DIAMONDS

Throughout this book we are going to use diamonds as a metaphor for dream clients.

And by dream clients I mean ones who value what you do, want every service they need from you, are prepared to pay top dollar for it, take action based on the advice you give them, give you all the data you need, in the format you need it, when you want it and who attract other clients just like them.

They're the ones you're secretly looking for when you fantasise about getting rid of the PITA clients, only to have your dreams dashed when you discover that this *new* client, who you thought would be a diamond, turns out to be just another PITA.

This is because of a simple fact that most people don't consider… diamonds don't look like diamonds.

Diamonds are rough lumps of rock with sharp jagged edges, buried in the ground and covered in dirt.

Yes, they may have a few sparkly bits, and that's the bit you fell in love with about them initially, BUT… they remained a dull, rough looking, sharp rock.

So, you keep looking.

But not only do diamonds not look like shiny, beautifully cut diamonds, they also don't just become one without some serious effort on **your** part.

Diamonds need to be dug out the ground, cleaned, shaped, cut and polished before they resemble a diamond, and that's YOUR responsibility to do that, not the rock's.

There are all these accounting businesses out there, desperately looking for diamond clients, and constantly being frustrated and despondent in their inability to find them.

But very few A) know what they're looking for, and therefore discard many worthy diamonds, and B) haven't developed the diamond polishing skills to turn these lumps of rock INTO diamonds.

I will train you in how to find and polish these diamonds.

And when you learn what you're *really* looking for, you will start to see they're all around you.

To sum up, I will:

- Enable you to see that what you're looking for, you already have
- Help you to understand that it exists in far greater abundance that you currently think
- Equip you with strategies to access this untapped potential
- Challenge your core beliefs and alter your mindset and with it, bring higher success

To do this, I'm going to have to take you on a roller-coaster with some unexpected twists, turns and dark tunnels that may be beyond the remit of what is effectively, a business book designed to help you to make a bit more cash.

I want this to make a genuine, lasting difference in your business and your life, so I can see no other effective route, other than the one we're going to go on; the same one I took those 100 firms on.

The order of this journey is going to be...

- Setting your goal so you know where you need to get to and why
- Understanding the depth of the problem you face and why it must be overcome... now!
- Why it's so hard to overcome this problem, especially for you, and discovering the fundamental shifts you have to make in your thinking and your life to succeed (heavy stuff)
- What it takes to make an immediate and lasting breakthrough

- How to prepare your thinking for massive success that will deliver profound results across all areas of your business and life
- The winning formula for how to increase fees with every client regardless of how difficult you may perceive that to be
- How to be courageous and overcome every obstacle you will face along the way

"Amazing Progress This Week"

'I've made amazing progress this week. 3 meetings so far, with fee increases of 69%, 132% and 210%!!! Mostly relating to work I was already doing but not charging for correctly.'

Gillian Caughey | Fearless Financials

TO THE BUSINESS OWNERS

This book is for any member of the team, whether you're on the front line serving the clients, in the leadership team, a partner or a firm owner.

But I just want to speak for a moment, to the owners of the business.

I have so much respect for anyone who sets up, owns and runs a business, with the intention of making their lives better and the lives of those people around them, whether that's their family, their team, their clients or others they're able to impact through their positive contributions to the world.

But building a business and achieving success is tough and will challenge you to the very core of your being.

People look at you and think that success is easy. Hell… *you* even thought success would be easy.

What people think success looks like

What success actually looks like

No-one will see the self-doubt, the tears, the late nights, the missed weekends, the sacrificed holidays, the arguments with loved ones, the risks you take or the earning of minimum wage… or less… for a long time.

No-one will share your vision of where you're going, and nor can you expect them to. That vision was created by you, for you, and you alone.

No-one else will believe in you until you make it, not even you, not really.

And when you do taste even the smallest amount of success and express that by taking a nice family holiday, buying a nicer car, a bigger house or working fewer hours, that's all other people see, and you feel guilty, despite what you've put in to get there.

But I **do** know what you go through.

I personally know the pains of building a business and the lows watching it fail.

I know the struggle of starting again with the self-doubt and judgement of others, that's even greater than the first time.

I know who I had to become to move through that, to build a business that delivers great impact to the clients we serve, inspires the team to flourish, runs entirely without me, paid me a significant salary and ultimately enabled me to sell it for a significant sum.

And the principles I've learned, strategies I've honed and mindset I've had to harness, are exactly what I shared with those 100 firms I worked with for those 30 days and the 1000's of firms I've helped to make significant breakthroughs, via GoProposal and my book "Selling to Serve."

I have written this new book to help you and I speak to you as a friend, as a fellow business owner, as a husband and as a father, to move you forward, by sharing the hard-fought learnings I've had on my journey.

This book will probably be nothing like you expected. This is not a standard business book. There will be times where you think... where is he going with this?

But please trust me.

The journey we are going to go on together is the journey I went on and the journey I've helped thousands of others to go on, with immediate and often dramatic results.

I congratulate you... for everything you're attempting, everything you've been through and everything you hope to be.

Well done for picking up this book and taking the time to devote to you, so that you may better serve others.

No-one deserves your time **more** than you.

I hope you get from it, **everything** you're looking for, and if you believe you might, then there's every chance you will.

"A Total Mindset Change"

'Crazy to think that I was commonly charging £87.50 per month for accounts. Now it's not uncommon to sign £1k per month. All thanks to a total mindset change.'

Jeri Williams | Smooth Accounting

A QUICK WORD ABOUT GOPROPOSAL

Throughout this book you are going to see mentions to GoProposal.

GoProposal is the onboarding software I developed to enable accounting businesses to price consistently, sell more confidently and minimise risk across their entire firm, and which, in 2021 was acquired by Sage.

You may use other software.

You may use an Excel spreadsheet to price and Microsoft Word to produce proposals and engagement letters.

You may use a finger in the air and a back of a cigarette packet.

Whatever you use, I wish you well.

Most of the stories I share are from GoProposal members as they're the ones I work closest with, and with whom it's been my passion to help succeed and who share their stories with me.

Right at the very end of the book, I will give you a brief and very factual explanation of the product, should you wish to consider it as an option for your accounting business. And if you don't, I wish you every success in implementing the strategies I am sharing, with whatever solution works best for you.

PART 1
THE GOAL

MAKE MORE MONEY

The primary function of your accounting business is to make money.

That's not to say it's your reason *why*; it might not be the thing that gets you out of bed in a morning. Your reason *why* might be to give you and your family the life you deserve, to give employment to your team, to boost the growth of small businesses, to improve the economy or to contribute to worthwhile causes.

But it's hard to do any of those things without money, so making money **is** the primary function, as cold as that may seem.

Nearly all the problems in your business can be traced back to the fact that you're not making enough money.

The fact that you're struggling to employ the right staff is because you can't afford to pay them the wages they need, because… you're not making enough money.

The reason you're not attracting a queue of dream clients wanting to do business with you is because you can't invest enough time or money into the proper marketing of your business because… you're not making enough money.

And money doesn't make you rich, it's what it enables, that will enrich your life.

I've had no money and I've had lots of money and I can do far more good in the world and positively impact more people's lives *with* money than without.

Money doesn't necessarily make you happy, but never having to worry about it, ever again, certainly does.

So, I'm good with the idea of making money and you should be too.

But how do you make more money? What are the only activities that generate more money in your business and how often are you focused on them? Do you know what they are, off the top of your head?

Because there are in fact only two things you can do to **make more money** in your accounting business...

...which is to **get more clients** or **give more value** to the clients you already have. That's it. They're the only two things that make you more money.

There are only two things you can do to **get more clients**...

… they are to **get more leads** or to **convert more** of those leads into clients.

There are only two things you can do to **give more value**…

… they are to **sell more to them** or to **increase the frequency** you're selling and providing current services, such as reviewing fees more regularly and moving *quarterly* management accounts to *monthly* or *monthly* bookkeeping to *daily*.

Now I know what you're thinking, 'what about **profit margin?'** Well absolutely, you can improve your profit margin, but that doesn't make your business more money, it only allows it to keep more of it, which is a good thing for sure.

There are only three ways you can improve your **profit margin**...

...which is to **reduce overheads**, **improve efficiencies** or **increase prices.**

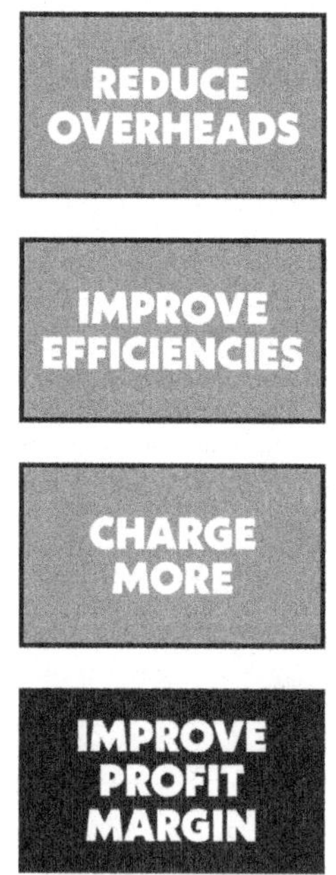

When you start to map all of these out together, you start to get a clear picture of what contributes to you making more money.

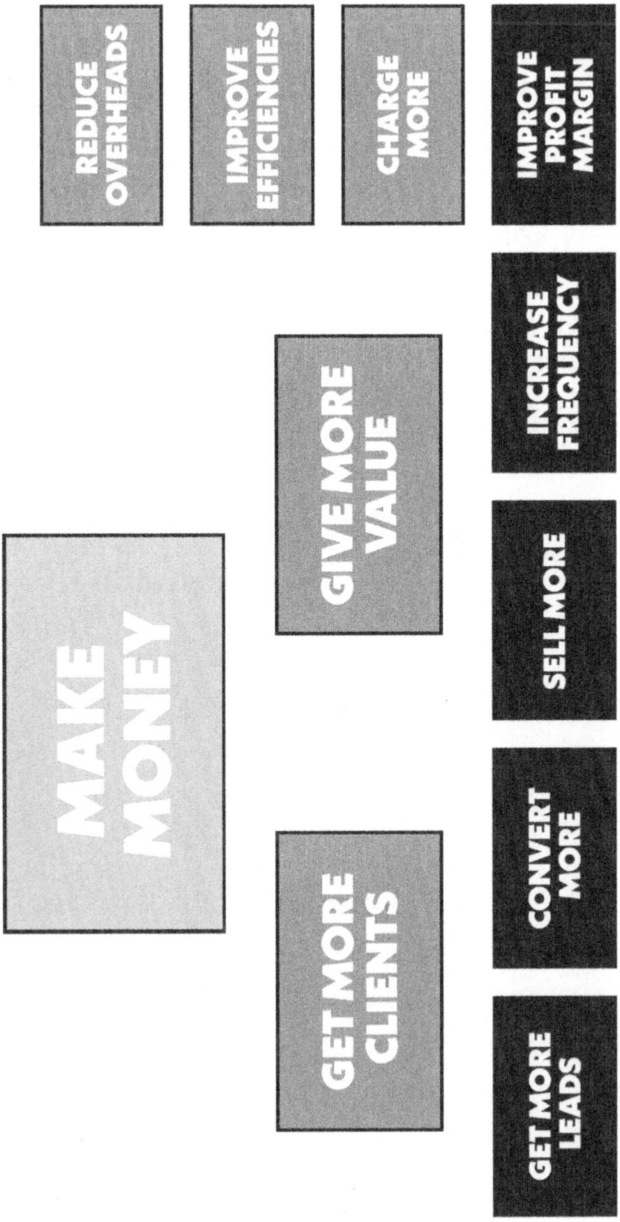

MAKE MONEY

GET MORE CLIENTS

GIVE MORE VALUE

GET MORE LEADS

CONVERT MORE

SELL MORE

INCREASE FREQUENCY

IMPROVE PROFIT MARGIN

CHARGE MORE

IMPROVE EFFICIENCIES

REDUCE OVERHEADS

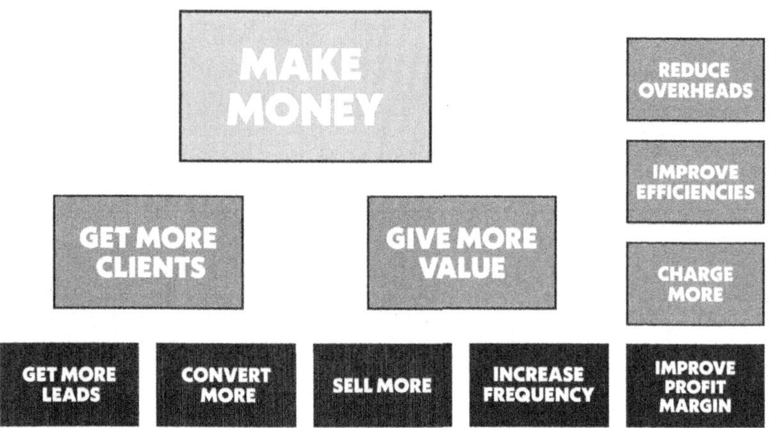

When I've shown this diagram to accountants and bookkeepers in the past, I've asked them which ones they tend to focus on, when attempting to make more money.

Their default answer tends to be '**reduce overheads.'**

And then they believe they will make more money if they could just **get more clients.**

The problem with **reducing overheads** is that it comes from a scarcity mindset, it's limited in how successful it can be and there's a tipping point when reducing them too far, becomes detrimental to achieving all the others.

And the problem with aiming to **get more clients** is that it takes time, it costs money, it's resource-heavy to onboard a new client and there are always a lot of unknowns.

Why try to fill a leaking bucket if you're not making all you can out of all you have? It makes no sense.

My question is: Out of all those areas you *could* focus on, which are the three that could have the most impact on your business in the shortest time?

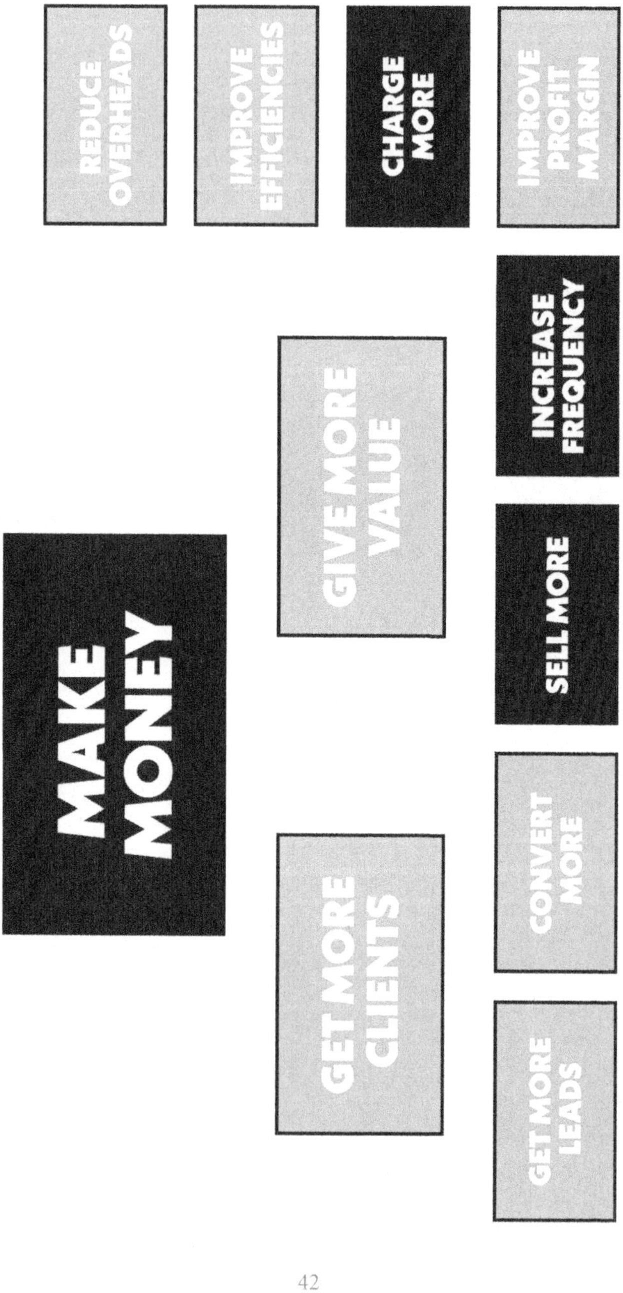

MAKE MONEY

GET MORE CLIENTS

GIVE MORE VALUE

GET MORE LEADS

CONVERT MORE

SELL MORE

INCREASE FREQUENCY

IMPROVE PROFIT MARGIN

CHARGE MORE

IMPROVE EFFICIENCIES

REDUCE OVERHEADS

The fastest way to make more money is to **charge more**, which is a combination of increasing prices and managing scope, to **sell more** to existing clients and to **increase the frequency** you sell and provide those services.

You know these clients, they're in your database, you don't need to onboard them.

Once you have improved those three areas by a significant amount, **then** you should spread your focus onto all the other areas.

The five black boxes below are all the activities you should be focusing on to make more money.

If you are focusing on anything else, then you are a cost to your business.

How much time are you spending on these activities? How could you spend more?

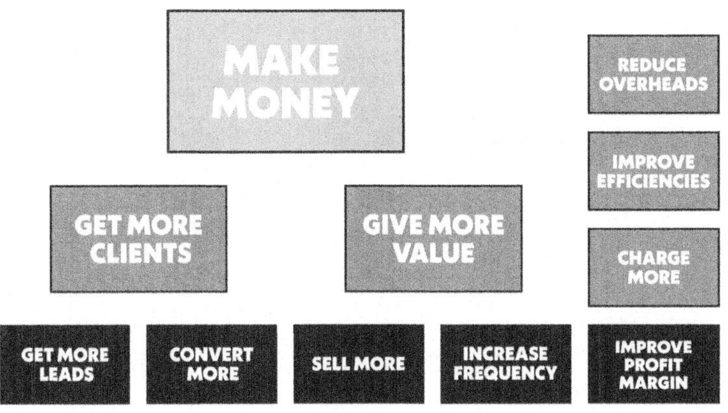

COMPOUNDING

There's a wonderful phenomenon you'll be familiar with, which is compounding.

If you can make small, incremental improvements in each area, you have an exponential impact on the amount of money you make.

A 10% increase in any of these areas doesn't seem impossible, right? But if you were to just improve each of the 5 black boxes by 10% (so 10% more leads, 10% better conversion rate, sell 10% more to existing clients, increase the frequency of those services by 10% and improve your profit margin by 10%), you would generate 61% more money, because of the magic of compounding.

And when I say increase your profit margin by 10%, if it's 20% now, I don't mean increase it to 30%, I mean increase it to 22%. It's just a 10% improvement. You could do that right?

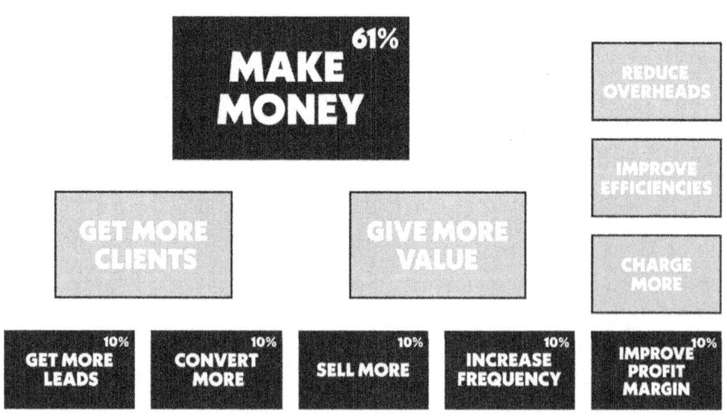

Even if we just focussed on the most immediately impactful areas – **selling more, increasing frequency** and **charging more.**

Even if you just increased each of those areas by 10%, you would make 33% more money. That is massive.

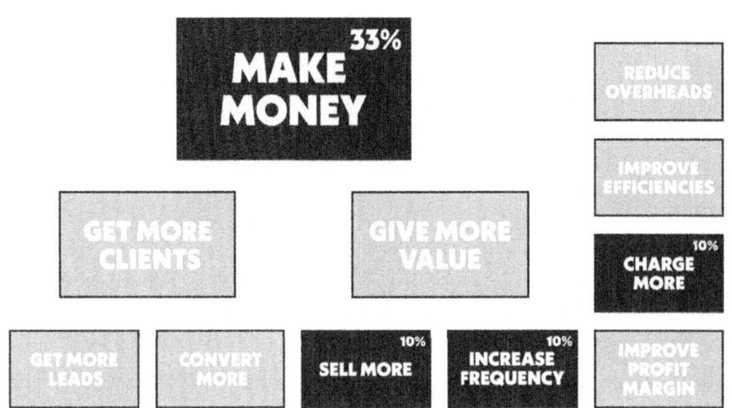

CLOUD 360 ACCOUNTING

There's a brilliant accounting business in Northern Ireland called Cloud 360 Accountanting, headed up by Kieran Phelan who is a great guy.

When I first met Kieran a few years ago, he knew all the principles around pricing and selling but they'd never quite clicked; the software he was using didn't do all the things it needed to do, his mindset wasn't quite right, and his team weren't on board.

It was a classic case of knowing what to do, but still not doing it.

But shortly before he encountered us, he'd had a health scare.

This health scare had forced him to re-evaluate his business and his life.

As a very family orientated person and a driven entrepreneur, he started to question why he was working so hard for so little and not spending as much time as he wanted with his family and doing the things he loved.

He adopted GoProposal and our philosophies and went for it.

He repriced his entire client base within 3 months.

During that time he lost 17% of his client base, including his cousin, who wasn't prepared to pay the increased fees. But Kieran wasn't prepared to put up with it any longer, from anyone.

By the end of those three months, despite losing 17% of his client base, he increased the amount of money he was making by 33%.

He was able to recruit new staff at a higher level.

He was able to pay himself more.

He was able to go from working 6 days a week to 4.

It was a massive breakthrough that positively impacted everyone around him, and all by making small, incremental improvements… fast.

The part I love about this story is that 12 months later his cousin returned and explained he'd made a huge mistake, asking if he could come back. And Kieran said he could but… his fees had increased again since he'd last quoted.

This time, he paid.

To add to the story, Kieran repriced his cousin's services again in March 2022, after not repricing during the pandemic. A small increase in services were delivered for another 33% increase in monthly fees.

THE ACCOUNTANT'S DEFAULT THINKING

I have hundreds of stories like Kieran's. Some you'll see throughout this book.

Over the years we have enabled accounting businesses all over the world to help *their* clients to invest into the finance function of their businesses at a much higher level and as a result, attract millions more into the accounting industry.

Forget the books and thousands of hours of video training we share with the world, GoProposal alone processes over £100million worth of won proposals each year. If you assume an average uplift of 20% in fees because of the software and our principles, that's an additional £20million we're helping to bring into the accounting industry... each year... and it's growing... rapidly.

This is why it pains me when I see accountants defaulting to **reducing overheads** in their business in order to save money, especially because it prevents them from making significantly more.

I've seen them reduce their software spend by £60 a month, which limits their ability to use it, or it reduces the number of users accessing the software, just to save a few pounds, which prevents them from having an army of people being able to drive their business forward.

And do you know why they default to this mode? Because that's what they were trained to do; it's their curse.

Throughout their accounting training, they're trained to look at ways they can help their clients to reduce overheads and minimise tax in order to save a few pounds.

They don't necessarily get trained in how to help their clients to massively increase their prices, to increase efficiencies, to sell more, to increase the frequency of selling and providing their services, to get more leads or to convert more.

They are trained to focus on the ONE area that is limited in its success (you can only save so much) and the only one that can negatively impact all the others.

But because that's what they've been trained in, they bring 'accountant' thinking to their own business rather than 'entrepreneur' thinking and in doing so, massively hinder their ability to succeed.

This entire book is based on the 100 firms I helped to grow their revenue, from existing clients, by £1million, in 30 days, from existing clients alone.

That's an average increase in fees of £833 per month… FROM EXISITING CLIENTS… FOR LARGELY THE SAME WORK THEY WERE ALREADY DOING.

Imagine if they continued to do that for 12 months?

On average, their fees would have increased by £10,000 per annum… and these were small firms.

If you're a small firm, tell me that an increase of £10k a year wouldn't change things!!!

And this all comes from having an abundant mindset and focussing on what's possible.

Then, with this additional revenue, imagine how you could improve your efficiencies through more staff, additional staff training, better processes and better systems.

Then, with a highly profitable, efficient machine, imagine starting to turn on the tap by investing in getting more leads and converting more of them into clients.

At that point, you would have created a growth machine that gives you **options** and that's what you want; options to scale, options to step back, options to keep it as it is, options to franchise, options to buy other firms, options to sell, options to invest in something else and diversify.

I see so many firms, struggling, with no options.

Just yesterday I heard of a leading accountancy firm here in the UK looking to buy another firm which they thought was profitable, but the firm wasn't accounting for the partners' salaries at a market rate, and when they rolled those in, it was barely breaking even.

It wasn't even worth the 1x fees they thought it would be. Their options were massively reduced.

You have no idea what the future holds so you must be in a position to be agile and have the greatest number of options so you can best respond to changes in the world, changes in the market or changes in your life circumstances. And your options start to increase when you charge more, sell more and make more money… not when you cut back and hunker down.

Your options start to increase when you charge more, sell more and make more money… not when you cut back and hunker down.

THE KNOCK-ON EFFECT

The beauty in thinking in this way, is that once you master it for yourself and start focussing on all these areas to make more money, guess what? You can help your clients to do the same.

I bet if I went on your website, it would say that one of the main ways you can help your clients is by reducing their overheads and minimising tax.

When you switch your focus to the other areas in YOUR business and start to make more money for yourself, you put yourself in a powerful position to help your clients to do the same.

Your clients are businesses too. The primary function of their businesses is to make money as well.

But how can you help them to do it if you can't first do it for yourself?

Imagine the change in conversation if you started talking to your clients about the prices they charge, how much they sell and the frequency of those sales. Imagine the impact you could have.

Focussing on making more money for your business is the most selfless thing you can do, because it enables you to help your clients to do the same.

DON'T LOOK BACK

When you make this breakthrough, you will have broken through; the ceiling that was holding you back will be gone.

This is achieved, even with a small win, a small fee increase.

The reason I say this is because it's likely you will start getting wins and you won't believe it, and not wanting to tempt fate, you start suggesting in your mind that it's only temporary.

I hear it in people's voices when I ask how things are going.

Things are going good… at the moment (implying it might change in the future.)

Well *that* fee review went well (implying the next one might not.)

Don't look back, or you'll go back.

You need to believe in the strategy and keep going.

That's not to say you won't hit bumps in the road, but they're just that, bumps, not roadblocks. But even if they were, as you build up speed, you'll just smash through them anyway.

If I ask you how things are going, say…

"Things are great and getting better."

If I ask you how the last fee review went, say…

"Brilliant and the next one will be better still."

Watch your words. Don't plant seeds of doubt, because the moment you encounter anything that reinforces that belief, fear will set in, and you may start to go back.

YOU ARE INCREDIBLE

Human beings are incredible.

We have figured out how to bend metal to construct airplanes and fly many tonnes through the air.

We've developed electricity and the electric light bulb.

We speak to each other via video from the other side of the world, making it possible to work from anywhere, consult with a physician or learn anything you want… in an instant… ON YOUR PHONE.

We've developed incredible breakthroughs in medicine that have saved billions of lives

Electric vehicles and innovations in solar and wind power are helping to save the planet.

Human beings are incredible. YOU… are incredible.

All we are talking about here is how to increase your revenue by £300 a month or £1,000 a month or £10,000 a month.

It's not such a daunting prospect.

Whatever it takes, we can do this… and we will.

We're going forwards, we're going up and when we hit obstacles, we're going through, up, around or over. They will not stop us.

PART 2
THE PROBLEM

UNTAPPED by JAMES ASHFORD

HOW BAD IS IT?

I've been through this process with many firms before and there's a point in the process where everyone is still sat there smiling, nodding along, making notes.

And I look at them thinking… 'Do you realise how bad this is?'

I then give them a scenario I'm about to give you and ask them to rate on a scale of **Not Ideal** to **This Fills Me with The Fear of God**, how it makes them feel.

Picture this: Let's say you're a super profitable firm and you make a 30% profit margin.

Then let's say you look at what fees you should be charging to achieve those margins and you pick out a specific client to see how they compare.

You realise that IDEALLY, you should be charging that client £180 a month, but in fact, you are ACTUALLY only charging them £153 a month… so just £27 off the pace.

How does that make you feel?

1	2	3	4	5	6	7	8	9	10

^ Not Ideal Fills Me with The Fear of God ^

Let's take a closer look. You are a business. The primary function of that business is to make money. If you are £27 off the pace, then you have in effect, halved the amount of money that client is generating you in terms of profit.

Because you see (and I know I'm teaching you to suck eggs here) you're not deducting the £27 from the £180, which doesn't sound that bad, you're deducting the £27 from the profit, from the £54 profit, and that sounds a whole lot worse.

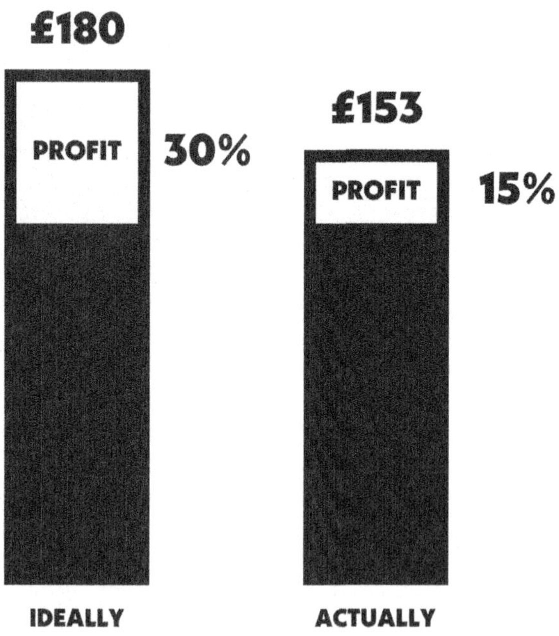

Do you know what that means in real terms?

You now need TWICE the number of clients to make the SAME amount of money. And you wonder why you're working so hard.

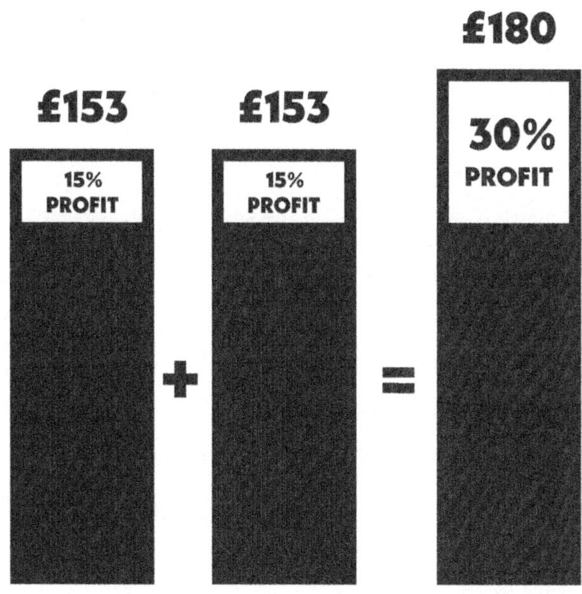

How does that make you feel now?

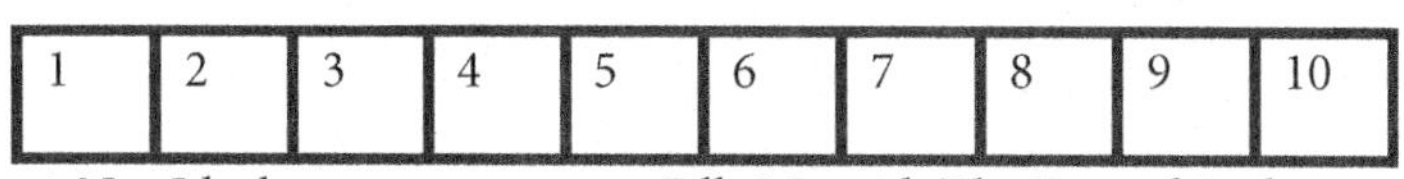

^ Not Ideal Fills Me with The Fear of God ^

I met with another firm today and they made a more realistic 20% profit margin.

I asked everyone in the room if they were faced with a client who they'd priced at £550, and that client said, "Look, if you do it for £500, I'll sign up now." How many of them would take on that client?

Half of them said, "Yes." Would you? It's only £50 off… for a £500 a month client.

OR… same scenario but painted in a different way. You've taken on a £500 a month client and over time, the workload had extended to be £550, but the fee had stayed the same. Would they see it as bad?

Well now you know the score. In your mind you deduct £50 from £550, and it doesn't seem too bad. But that's not what's happening. You're taking £50 off the £110 profit and that is bad; it's devastating.

Again, that little iddy biddy £50 deduction in fees, or a £50 growth in the scope, means you now need almost twice as many clients.

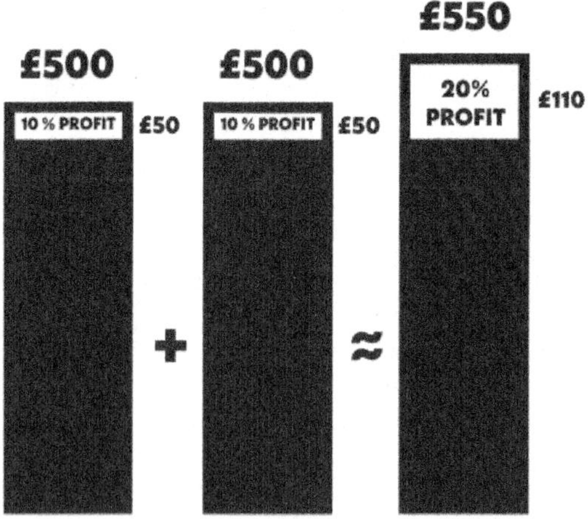

At first glance, it doesn't seem so bad and it's totally forgivable as to why this picture doesn't force you into immediate action.

But when you look more closely and extrapolate that idea across your entire client base, you start to paint a very dire picture indeed, and the knock-on effect can be devastating.

I know of firms who have such low staff morale that sickness records are through the roof and they can't recruit people. It's all because the clients don't value the work that's being done because the staff can't perform at a high enough level and the resources are being stretched and the underlying reason is that they're just not making enough money.

The bucket is leaking and rather than fix the leaks, they just try to fill the bucket faster.

The work becomes demoralising.

They have to get cheaper and cheaper labour.

Corners get cut.

Fines start to appear.

Clients ask for discounts.

Money dries up so they try to bring in more and more clients at low rates and the problems get worse.

If they just stopped... sealed the leaks and restored the profit margins, they could raise the level of service, attract the staff at the right level and pay them more. They could invest in staff training, improve the culture and create the optimum environment for them to do their best work.

They could invest in systems and processes and technology to improve efficiencies.

And when this happens, the team start to love what they're doing and produce work that the clients value.

You see it's not about the money, but rather what the money enables or restricts.

If you can't control your profitability, you can't control anything else.

"He accepted the proposal in 12 MINUTES"

'Holy cannoli - fee increase from £1000 to £1476! Minor increase in services (which was all stuff that we were already doing due to scope creep) AND he accepted the proposal in 12 MINUTES.'

Carolyn Burchell | Composure Accounting & Taxation

IT'S ALL ABOUT PROFIT

You have to become obsessed about profit.

You know the old adage… revenue for vanity and profit for sanity.

This shift in focus will make you sane.

To understand the scale of the problem and set some clear outcomes, we have to analyse your current client base.

I'm going to do this across 3 broad scenarios.

SCENARIO B

Let's say your firm makes the more modest 20% profit and you have a client who pays you £100 a month INITIALLY.

But EVENTUALLY, over time, their business has grown, they have more staff, you have more interactions with them, and you do more work for them, to the point where you are now only just breaking even.

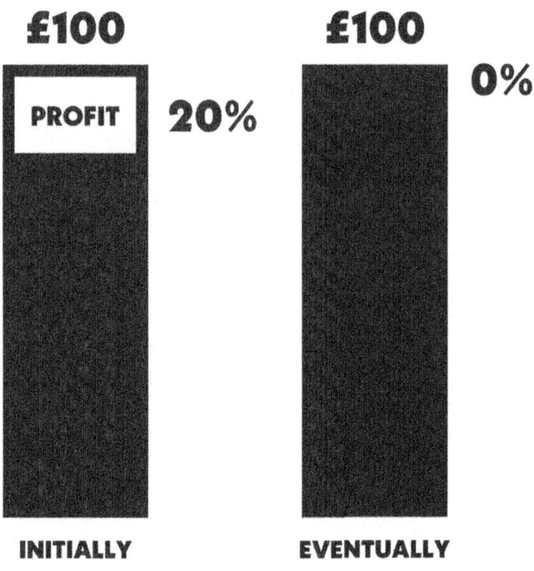

IDEALLY, you would have to raise their fee to £125 a month, just to restore your profit margin. And that £25 increase in fees is now pure profit for you. This should not be too difficult a conversation to have, but would make a huge difference to you.

SCENARIO C

But what's PROBABLY also happening, is that you have clients where you're doing so much work for them and have failed to increase their fees for so long, that you're making a LOSS with those clients.

So it's COSTING you money to keep those clients, and they're the ones you're stressing about losing!!! It would actually *save* you money if you were to let them go.

If you're now doing £110 a month worth of work for them, but they're only paying £100 a month, you would have to raise their fee to £132 a month to restore the 20% profit margin OR, you'd have to significantly reduce the work you're doing for them. But doing one of these steps with some sense of urgency is CRITICALLY important.

They can either keep having what they're having, or they can keep paying what they're paying, but they can't have both.

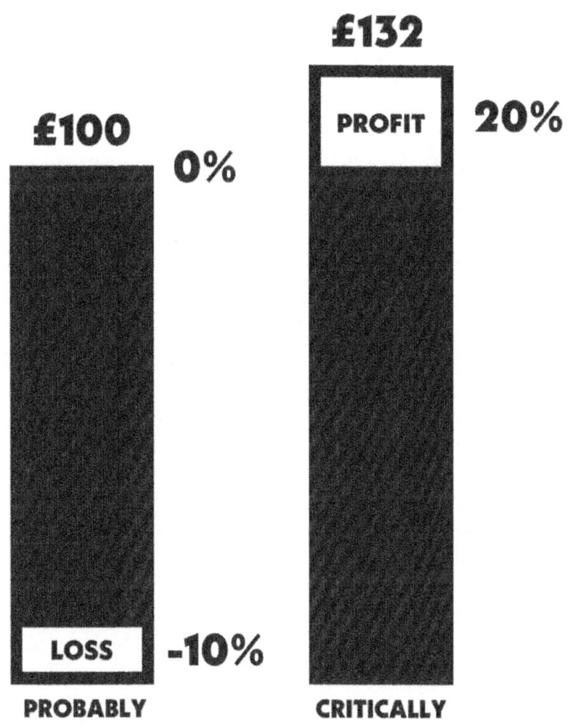

WHERE'S SCENARIO A?

Scenario A is what I hope you also have, which are clients who are profitable and enabling you to hit your profit margin.

These require a different conversation.

You don't need to charge these clients more, but you probably have a lot of scope to serve them to higher levels.

These clients want so much more from you and may be willing to spend 10 times more with you, if you were just able to do all you could for them.

But the reason you're not able to do that is because of all the time you're wasting on scenario C clients.

You need to sit with these clients and present to them everything you would want, if you were them, knowing what you know. Not 75% of what you would want, but 100% of what you would want.

They don't have to take it all, but you are not being fair to them if you don't at least present your very best level of service to these clients.

HOW MANY A, B & C's DO YOU HAVE?

The first step is for you to figure out how many As, Bs and Cs you have…

A – Assets for your business

B – Breaking even

C – Costing you money

When I've done this exercise before, in the absence of a consistent pricing system that is being used on a regular basis by the majority of your team… you will find that a third of your clients will be As, a third will be Bs and a third will be Cs.

There's rarely anymore science needed than that.

You need to establish your current client position and it only needs to be approximate for the purpose of what we're going to do.

At the end of the day, you need to reprice your entire client base and you could do that over a 12-month period as their year ends present themselves OR you could be much more aggressive and tackle this over a shorter time frame.

If you were to tackle it quicker, you may wish to do it more strategically.

You may choose to tackle the C's first because they are costing you money and even if you were to lose some of them, you would be better off. This will massively free up your time and headspace.

You may wish to tackle A's next, because these represent the greatest opportunity to significantly grow your revenue in a short time and you will now have the time and capacity to serve them.

Then you may wish to process the B's as their year ends appear, over the next 12 months.

It's up to you.

Just know this...

- They all need recalibrating.
- The longer it goes on, the worse the situation gets
- You have to do it at some point, so why not sooner?

To help you to detach from this decision emotionally, the question to ask yourself is... **If you just bought this business today, what bold decisions would you make?**

BREAKTHROUGH ACTIVITY

Get a list of all your clients and categorise them into A's, B's and C's.

It only needs to be a rough approximation if you don't have any data to support your split. I would even take a gut feel for now.

"We have made an extra £32k fees"

'We finally got round to quoting every client for the services they need but more importantly want to achieve their goals - only 10% in and we have made an extra 32k fees - why oh why did I wait?

As always, thank you for the motivation and support.'

Stephen Paul | Valued

AGREE YOUR OUTCOME

I'm hoping you're starting to get a sense of the scale of the problem. You don't need to know how to fix it at this stage, just know there's a burning issue that needs to be solved.

It's going to take time to solve it all and you may have to marshal the efforts of your team to achieve that, but we need to make a start.

Remember, this book isn't about sharing nice ideas, this book is about making a difference, otherwise why read it?

I want you to think about what financial outcome you would love to achieve over the next 30, 60 or 90 days.

What amount of additional revenue would make a difference to you and would give you the confidence that your business can be transformed?

For example, you may put, 'Today is the **1st June** and over the next **30** days I am going to grow my monthly recurring revenue by **£500** from **existing** clients.'

I would much rather this be from **existing clients** so I can prove what a diamond mine you're sat on, but you may have a valid reason why this isn't possible, such as you're a new business with no clients. So ONLY if you have a valid reason can you put **new clients** in that section.

And don't be afraid to set the bar low. I'm all for shooting for the stars and if you miss, you'll at least hit the moon. But I'm more interested in making sure you get off the ground for now.

We can always build on the goal next month and the month after that.

Once you know your intended OUTCOME, you need to know your reason WHY.

WHY is this important for you to achieve?

WHY should this be a priority?

WHY does this deserve your focus?

When you hit bumps in the road on this journey, this is the statement you're going to need to push through. And as you write this, make sure your words are precise, strong and compelling.

If your reason why is *'because I'd like to earn a bit more cash and have some more free time with the family'*... it won't work. It's not compelling enough AND if you raised your income by £5 a month and knocked off work at 5:55pm on a Friday instead of 6:00pm, you would have achieved your *why*.

So make it strong and make it compelling.

For example, is your reason why...

'Because I'm sick to death of working Saturday mornings and missing my kid's football practice, because we're not getting through the work in the week because the clients aren't paying us enough for me to be able to afford that next member of staff. So this must change now.'

Now it's time to commit to *your* outcome and *your* reason why.

Today is the ____________________ and over the next ________ days I am going to grow my monthly recurring revenue by_____________ from _____________ clients.

The reason why this must become my #1 priority right now and deserves my full focus is because ____________________

____

____

____

____

____

____

____

____

____

Once you have made this commitment to your outcome and your reason why to yourself, I want you to make it to someone else too. We will let ourselves down before we're prepared to let someone else down.

Take a photo of that page and send it to your partner, your mum, your dad, your best friend, your team, whoever you trust to champion this, but who also loves you enough to hold you to the flame and to challenge your progress each week.

Tell them that this is an important commitment you are making to yourself and you are sharing it with them because you know it will make a real difference in your business and your life when you achieve it.

Ask them if they will hold you to account, to following through with your commitment and to give you some tough love if needed.

Tell them not to accept any BS excuses from you. This MUST happen and it must happen now.

I also want you to write it out or tear the page out of the book and put it up in a place where you can see it every day such as your fridge door, front door, bathroom mirror or car dashboard.

The next thing I need you to do is to set up a spreadsheet (I know how much you love spreadsheets.)

And create these headings (or something similar) along the top.

Identified Clients	Current Fee	Target Increase in Fees	Fee Review Completed	Fee Review Accepted	Actual Increase in Fees	Actual Increase as a % of target

This is how you're going to track your progress over the next 30, 60 or 90 days.

Give your team access to this.

Have it up on a screen for everyone to see every day, not hidden on a file on your laptop.

If you want to grab a copy of an Excel sheet already filled out with the formulas, then you can get it from www.goproposal.com/untapped, as well as the other resources that accompany this book. Alternatively, you can scan this QR code and it will take you straight there.

RECAP

- Even small reductions in fees can have huge corrosive effects on your profitability and therefore workload
- You need to fully understand the scale of the problem and the order in which you're going to tackle it
- You can be strategic about how you solve this situation, but know this…
    - They all need recalibrating
    - The longer it goes on, the worse the situation gets
    - You have to do it at some point, so why not sooner?
- You need to get clear on your outcome and have sight of that every day
- You need to get clear on your reason why, to push you through
- You need to track your progress and ideally to have someone who will help to hold you to account

PART 3

WHY IT'S SO HARD TO SOLVE

A LACK OF ABUNDANCE

To recap on what I said at the start of the book, what 'abundance thinking' says, is… there *is* enough of everything I want around me already, I *am* capable of getting it, I deserve to get it and I will do whatever it takes *until* I get it.

Now that may be money, but it may also be time, joy, fulfilment, love, connection, clients, whatever it means to you.

But whatever that is for you, whatever it is that you *really* want, you are capable of getting it, you deserve to get it, there's enough of it within reach, and you can get it.

That is abundant thinking.

What 'scarcity thinking' says is… there is not enough of what I need out there, so I need to hold onto what I have so I don't lose any more and the more I see other people get what *they* want, the less there will be for me in the future.

Again, that may be money, but it may also be time, joy, fulfilment, love, connection or clients.

Whatever it is that you want, there *isn't* enough, it's getting less all the time, so the best chance you have is to cling on dearly to what you have.

That is scarcity thinking.

I am an abundant thinker.

If I see someone with a nice car, I immediately think wow, what a beautiful car, the fact that this person can get a nice car is proof that I can get a nice car too.

Other people's successes spur me on to achieve greater success myself.

In fact, I will go out of my way to congratulate people on their achievements.

A neighbour recently got a new Porsche, so I stopped my car and knocked on his door to tell him what a beautiful car he had and congratulated him on putting in the hard work to get it.

Giving that positivity and praise to the world, actually gives back in many ways. I don't lose anything by doing that.

A scarcity thinker would see someone in a nice car and be immediately upset, because there's now one less nice car in the world for them to get, which worsens their situation, and they would likely believe there were large amounts of luck involved in them getting it.

When people believe that someone else's achievement was down to luck, what they're actually saying is that there was an external force at play, that got them that thing. Thereby implying that the only reason *they* haven't got what *they* want yet, is because they haven't been blessed with such luck (external factor) rather than admit that they haven't put in the work to get there.

Scarcity thinkers rarely accept responsibility for their situation. It's always somebody or something else's fault, like the client's or the economy's or the pandemic's or a lack of luck.

Remember, no-one has achieved anything of any note, without tremendous amounts of hard work, projected in one direction, continually, for a long period of time.

There are many reasons why it is better for you to have an abundant mindset as opposed to one of scarcity, but one largely unknown reason is that if you're in scarcity mode, I guarantee you're projecting this onto your clients and those around you.

We don't see the world as it is, we see the world as we are.

We project our view of the world onto others, and we don't even realise how we're doing it or *that* we're doing it.

For example, if you have a partner and all you see is everything about them that annoys you, I promise you that all they will start seeing in you, is everything that annoys them.

You get back exactly what you put out. This is a universal truth, as true as gravity.

So, if you start to see in them, everything you love about them, miraculously, they start to see everything they love about you.

To get the thing you most want, you need to give it first.

If you want to feel significance, make other people feel significant and it will come back to you.

If you want to feel love, make other people feel loved and it will come back to you.

If you want your clients to see **you** as a fantastic investment that will move their business forward, you've got to stop seeing the services, products and software that **you** spend money on as costs, but rather as great investments that will move your business forward.

And the moment you make that shift in your thinking, you will be amazed to see how the thinking changes in those around you.

"The thing you want the most of… is the very thing you're going to have to give the most of."

Steve Harvey | American TV Presenter

If you see the world through a lens of abundancy, believing there **is** enough and you **have** enough, your clients will start seeing you in the same way.

And likewise, if you start seeing the world through the lens of scarcity, believing you **don't** have enough and there **isn't** enough, guess what?

Don't ask me how it happens, but it does.

If you want to do more, achieve more and be more, you have to start thinking of more, not less.

"It dwarfed all my other fees entirely"

'The best example I've experienced of an abundance v scarcity mindset disparity between two potential clients happened last May in the space of 24 hours.

The first client had received a quote for services, we'd chatted loads about it and I play football with him every week too. Thought everything was in the back of the net! The proposal fee was much less than £100 per month yet he told me that was too high and he'll just do it all himself. I couldn't quite understand - I asked myself, "how much does he think an accountant should cost if that price was too high?"

The next day, I had a discovery/proposal call with a referred client and I was going in blind. She had a decent-sized business, and I was so nervous because the proposal came in at over roughly £1300 per month (plus VAT). It dwarfed all of my other fees entirely. The client signed up on the spot, and since then I like to think we've formed a great relationship, and I've also managed to increase that fee even more. This particular client always looks on the bright side of life. She had a £40K tax bill from her Self-Assessment which we randomly ending up having a big laugh about (albeit with a hefty number of expletives).

I think it takes a bit of practice to become an abundant thinker. Perhaps we are all naturally scarcity thinkers because of our primal instincts. All I know is that I don't want to be like the client who turned me down for a tiny fee, and I've been guilty of it many times in other areas of my life, all throughout my life. So it's time to recalibrate, and flip that abundant mindset for good.'

Andrew Evans | Sky Life Accountancy

THE MATTHEW PRINCIPLE

There is another hugely important reason why you need an abundant mindset and start moving towards what you want to achieve, with the conviction that you can achieve it, and that's because of something called the **Matthew Principle.**

It originates from the Bible and is commonly used in modern psychology.

The Matthew Principle states…

To those who have everything, ***more*** *will be given.*

And to those who have nothing, ***everything*** *will be taken.*

This seems harsh, but there is an undeniable truth to it.

Basically, if your situation is bad, it will get worse, and if you allow it to get worse, the chance of it getting MUCH worse in the future increases… exponentially.

The closer you get to get to the edge, the greater the possibility of you going over the edge becomes.

Think about it. Think about something that's happened in the past. It knocks your confidence, and you start to doubt yourself. You tell people about it and breathe more energy into it and you attract people who console you. You now become more wary of something else going wrong, so you start to obsess over avoiding mistakes and the more you focus on things going wrong, the more chance they have of *going* wrong. This dents your confidence further and down the spiral you go.

Conversely, as you move forward and your situation starts to improve, the chances of you making another improvement, increases also.

And again, this is not a linear growth, this is an exponential growth.

With each step you take, the chances of the next step being better, just keeps increasing.

Something good happens, your confidence boosts, your energy lifts, you start thinking and talking of progress, you start to resonate with people who think the same and you start to look for more opportunities for growth. Your confidence grows further and upwards you go.

Standing still is also not an option, because if you're just standing still as everything around you gets better, you are in fact, getting worse.

So, we have to actively try to move forward.

But sometimes, the reason people don't make any progress, is because they haven't **set the bar low enough.**

You have to be able to give yourself a fighting chance of getting the first win, because the chance of you getting the next win immediately becomes greater.

It's not about achieving great success, it's just about stopping the downward spiral and reversing the process initially, as we start to build momentum upwards.

I see firm owners being overwhelmed at the prospect of repricing all their clients because they realise they're massively undercharging, and because it's such a large project, they don't do it.

By not making a decision they decide to stay as they are.

But as I've said, standing still is not an option.

You have to imagine you're always standing on a moving escalator, facing the wrong way.

If you stand still, you go backwards.

If you choose to do nothing about all your underpaying clients, your situation is only going to get worse. And the more it goes on, the worse it's going to get.

If it's a level 3 problem today, it will be a level 4 problem next quarter, and a level 6 problem the quarter after that.

The way to turn it all around, is not to be daunted by the mountainous task of repricing all your clients, but just to reprice one… an easy one.

If you reprice a £50 a month client to £56 a month, it's a win.

You've gotten over the low bar.

Wahoo!!!

Now when you reprice the £60 a month client, you might get them to £83 a month.

Then you might get the £70 a month client to £126 a month.

What's your low bar? What's the first step?

DECISIONS NOT CONDITIONS

We've all had a crap hand dealt to us at some point in our life.

Your parents may have divorced when you were young.

You might have been born in a council house, to a single parent and had no money.

You may have left school with no qualifications.

You may have lost someone very close to you.

You might have had a business fail and lost everything.

Your business partner might have shafted you.

You might have lost your best member of staff and he took your best clients with him.

You might have had half your clients get wiped out when COVID-19 hit.

Shit happens.

But as Tony Robbins says, it's your **decisions,** not your **conditions,** that determine your success.

I know people that fit into some or all of the criteria above, who are hugely successful... multi-millionaires in some cases... because of the **decisions** they made.

You see, when something bad happens that's outside of your control, you **always** have a choice you can make... to be bitter, or to be better.

That choice always belongs to you, regardless of what happens.

MY STORY (THE ONE YOU DON'T KNOW)

I've always been an abundant thinker.

I did very well at school; straight A's (in the things I liked doing.)

I was the only person to have got 100% in their math's exam, because I focused on getting it and believed I could.

I got A's at A-Level.

I went onto complete a degree and master's degree in Product Design.

I got 93% for my degree and I later found out that the tutors had actually marked my work at 100%, but because they'd never awarded that to any student before, they didn't know what the implications would be, so they gave me 93% instead, which they thought I'd be happy with. I was.

I had strong academic success. I won awards, appeared in national papers and some of my work got on TV.

I thought I would leave academia and continue on that trajectory... but I didn't.

My first piece of furniture design I got manufactured failed, because it had been poorly made by the company and all fell apart.

My main design project from university was ripped-off by a large manufacturer and I started to blame my university for not giving me the protection or guidance I needed.

I started teaching art in the local prisons near me, which was a great learning experience and paid the bills.

I then moved to London to be a close-up magician, and that didn't pay the bills, so I became a waiter.

I setup a marketing agency that failed.

I blamed the client who didn't pay us.

I blamed the staff for not doing good enough work.

I blamed my accountant for not giving me the financial insights I needed to make informed decisions.

I blamed my bank for encouraging me to take a loan that was personally guaranteed against our house.

I blamed my parents for all the things they *failed* to give me. Hell, I even thought the fact I was brought up on Little-worth Lane, had something to do with it.

I blamed my wife for not supporting me in the way I thought she should.

I blamed other business opportunities I'd become involved in, which I thought had distracted me.

My business was spiralling down and there was nothing I could do about it because it was everybody else's fault.

I begrudged other people who seemed to be ahead of me, because I felt I should be further ahead than I was.

Years previously at university I'd started smoking cannabis, which was just a recreational thing to do at the time, but it had always lurked in the background of my life.

As my situation started to worsen and my internal pain increased, I started to lean on it more and more.

Pain is a curious thing.

Pain can be a gift if viewed in the right way.

As a lobster grows its shell becomes too small and it becomes painful.

When the pain gets to a certain point, that's the sign for the lobster to shed its shell, crawl under a rock and grow a larger one that it can now grow into… until **that** one becomes too small and induces pain and the cycle repeats.

You see, emotional pain can often be a sign that something needs to change; something needs to be left behind and something new needs to be created.

That's how someone operating above the line, sees pain. They see it as a trigger to grow and to be better.

I was way below the line, so rather than use the pain to grow, I tried to dull it with the only means I knew would work… cannabis.

I would make any excuse to leave the house early so I could start.

I would work through the day and come up with reasons why I needed to work late so I could prolong its numbing effects for as long as I could, before returning home.

My situation only got worse, and I continued to spiral down.

I split up with my wife and left the family home to live in a flat on my own.

I stopped seeing the joy in the world.

I had little gratitude for the things around me.

The business failed.

I was in debt.

The house I still shared with my wife had to be re-mortgaged.

I had tried everything to stop smoking and there were bouts when I did. But it would only expose the pain and what was lacking, so I would quickly return.

I tried hypnotherapy, psychotherapy, counselling and read leading literature on it but nothing seemed to work.

A friend of mine reached out and invited me to an event. This event was by Tony Robbins called 'Unleash the Power Within.'

It all seemed a bit happy-clappy when I checked it out online, but I had nothing to lose… literally.

My friend paid for me to attend and at that event, Tony Robbins helped me to make the breakthrough I desperately needed.

Being addicted to cannabis, something I'd been struggling with for almost 14 years, ended that day.

It was like I was picked up off a path that had ever-increasing pain ahead for me and those around me, and I was placed on a new one that would move everything forward in the most positive of ways.

I learned so many things over those few days and I saw for the first time, the possibility of life being lived on a whole new level.

I saw where I'd been going wrong.

You see, we all choose ways to numb the pain, whether that's smoking, alcohol, gambling, shopping, eating, promiscuity, prescribed medication or a raft of other vices.

We become addicted... not to the thing… but to the temporary removal of the pain it brings.

And at the bottom of that addiction is one question we ask ourselves… **am I enough?**

This doesn't have to be something we ask aloud, but in moments of quiet desperation, we ask ourselves… am I enough?

And the moment you start to ask yourself this question… you… this incredible human being who is capable of so much… who's very chance of being alive is 14 trillion to one, who's heart beats 100,000 times a day, who has the world's most powerful computer in their head, who's been given an amazing gift of this wonderful body, who is living in the best time in human history in terms of basic needs being met, safety and the scale of opportunity in front of you… if you doubt whether this most incredible creation… aka YOU… is enough… it's a very simple and logical step to then conclude… IS there enough?

Because surely if you're not enough, then there isn't enough; there can't be.

With two simple questions, you are plunged into scarcity thinking and you need something to stop that spiralling down and to reverse the direction upwards.

Now, I'm not saying for a second that you are at the low point I arrived at. But I want to share with you, the process I went through to stop my spiralling down, change my direction of travel and to arrive at where I am today, which is living an abundant life in every sense of the word.

"And to think I was so worried about it"

'Woooohooo. Two more accepted. £500 increase in monthly fees between them and they said that it was very reasonable. And to think I was so worried about it.

I also bit the bullet and told my biggest client that we need to discuss their renewal, that's £500 extra a month (currently on £2k) and we have that booked in too. This is fun!!'

Nicola Hageman | The Numbers Quarter

THE SIX NEEDS

What I learned at the event was that there are 4 primary needs we all must satisfy and 2 higher needs. The primary needs are…

#1 THE NEED FOR CERTAINTY

We need to know that our basic needs are being met; that we have a roof over our head, food to eat and money to support ourselves. We all have a need for certainty.

#2 THE NEED FOR UNCERTAINTY

We need to mix things up and have some excitement in our lives.

Your nature will determine how much certainty versus uncertainty you need in your life. You may need a steady, predictable life and be happy with one or two holidays a year. You may need to go white water rafting every week and live life more on the edge.

But whatever your make-up, you are satisfying both needs in proportions that work for you.

May I suggest at this point, that accountants, by their nature, have a natural proclivity towards certainty, which is what perhaps led you into this profession in the first place. And I'm not saying for a second that accountants can't go white-water rafting.

#3 THE NEED FOR SIGNIFICANCE

We all need to feel a sense of importance, that we're worth something to someone.

#4 THE NEED FOR LOVE, OR CONNECTION

We want to feel that we belong, that we're part of something and we're connected to that.

You are satisfying all of these needs in your life and here's the thing… you are either satisfying them in a positive way or a negative way, but you *are* satisfying them.

When I smoked, I was satisfying all of those needs in a negative way.

I had the certainty of the rituals I had to go through, the feeling it would give me and the removal of my pain.

I had the uncertainty of my thinking and how my mind would react.

I had the significance of feeling that I could do what I wanted, when I wanted, while others were working their 9-5's.

I had the connection of the people I did it with and what it stood for.

The problem then, is that if you remove the crutch and fail to satisfy those needs in a *positive* way, you will either move onto another vice or else fall back on the ones you know work.

And here's the key thing to know… if you can't satisfy those needs in a positive way, there is no way you can move onto the final two, higher needs which provide all the joy and fulfilment in life.

Anger is a simple way to satisfy significance. People who come home and shout at their kids or kick the dog, gain instant importance through that anger or violence.

People who are always coming to you with drama or their problems, gain significance by how *insignificant* they feel or by the size of their problems.

But we must learn to satisfy these needs positively so we can reach the highest level of the final two needs, and they are…

#5 THE NEED FOR GROWTH

Developing ourselves, learning and becoming stronger.

#6 THE NEED FOR CONTRIBUTION

Becoming more valuable to more people in the world.

When I made my breakthrough, I started on a journey of continual growth.

I'd read two books up until that point in my life. After that moment, I started reading a book a week.

I consumed audiobooks and watched inspirational and motivational videos. I invested in training and mentorship so I could continually learn and develop and become the best I could be.

And then I wanted to share and give it all back by contributing to others, so that they could grow and flourish too.

It was at this juncture in my life where I was faced with the decision of what to do next.

My business had gone, and I was back at the start.

I asked myself, what would I choose to do, even if I knew I couldn't get paid for it?

I made the conscious decision to help others to make the same breakthrough I'd made, especially those in business who were perhaps facing similar challenges to the ones I'd faced.

I wanted to help people to become more successful in their business and their life.

WHO'S IN YOUR CORNER?

One of the big things that helped me through this period and to succeed on the other side, were the people in my corner.

They say you are the average of the five people you spend the most time with.

I became very intentional about who I was spending time with and who was in my corner.

Through my friend and mentor, Paul Scanlon, I discovered that there are three types of friends…

The first two are those who are **for you** and those who are **for what you are for.**

You could have a business partner who you think is **for you** and who wants what's best for you, but they don't. They're **for what you are for**, i.e., that business being successful. The moment you're both not working towards the success of that business, they're no longer around because they were never for you.

You could have a friend who you think is for you, but it's conditional on you behaving in a certain way. And the moment you don't behave in that way, you realise they're not actually for you, but you being a certain way.

There are very few people who are genuinely **for you**: who love you as you are, regardless of what you do or don't do, or where you live, whether you spend time together or not.

If you can count 5 friends who are like this, then you're doing very well in life.

Friends who fall in the third type are those who are **against what you are against.**

These tend to be fewer but still worth knowing and the most subtle way they turn up, is when things are going wrong for you.

They're not really **for you**, or **for what you are for**, but when things go wrong, they will be quick to console you and be **against the thing you're against**, which could be debt, failure, illness etc...

But the moment things start to go good again, they disappear, because they were never really **for you** or **for the thing you are for**.

Just make a mental note to be wary of these people, because while they may seem to be supportive in your times of hardship, if they're ONLY there in those times, it's like they WANT things to go wrong for you and you can easily get sucked into a downward spiral of woe.

My main point here is for you to identify the people who are genuinely for you and to nurture those relationships.

One of the main people I had in my corner when I was growing up was a teacher from secondary school.

His name was Jonty and he loved magic, which is what brought us together as friends and kept us close over the years.

He landed me my first magic gig as a magician and was someone who was genuinely for me.

We became the best of friends and he's the only person to have visited me everywhere I've lived in my life, through all my ups and downs and stupid moments and never once judged me. He was always just for me.

Whenever we'd go out for a meal, he'd always pay, saying, "You'll be a millionaire one day, you can pay for me then."

Then one day while teaching at school he started getting headaches and passed out in class.

They rushed him to hospital and operated immediately, to discover two very aggressive brain tumours. They did what they could, but within 18 months he died, leaving his wife and two young children behind.

He was just 49 when he died.

I was privileged to be invited to give the eulogy at his funeral which was packed out with family, friends and students he'd impacted over the years.

People had to stand outside and watch it on TV screens because there were so many in attendance.

One of the lines I read was, "You don't have to change the world, just somebody's world, and Jonty certainly changed many people's world."

He contributed so positively and so beautifully to so many people's lives, genuinely championing them to being the best they could be.

He was **for**, so many people and through him, I have forged many lifelong friendships with people who are all for each other.

He showed me a level of love and friendship that very few people exude, with no judgement, expecting nothing in return, to be continually giving energy and lighting people up.

And through this he taught me a very valuable lesson, which at first will seem very bleak, but I do not mean it to be bleak in anyway.

So, I say these five words with love and kindness and positivity…

… **you are going to die.**

YOU ARE GOING TO DIE

I told you we'd be going on a journey with some unexpected twists and turns and dark tunnels.

This is one, but which has great brightness at the end.

The route I'm taking you on will get you to the precise point you need to be. But if we don't make some detours and specific stop-offs on the way, you won't be able to do the things you'll need to do when we get there.

Trust the process.

The fact that you are going to die, is your greatest gift.

I speak to so many firm owners who are afraid of putting fees up, afraid of upsetting a client, afraid of perhaps losing a client, afraid of getting something wrong, afraid of being less than perfect, afraid of failing and I want to say... why are you getting so concerned about all this when... you are going to die... and not only that... everyone you know is going to die too?

It's a hugely sobering thought that provides tremendous perspective.

We don't know how many laps of the sun we're going to get, but we do know that one of them will be our last.

So why stress about all the little bumps in the road on those laps? In the grand scheme of things, repricing a client, possibly upsetting a client, or losing a client is wholly irrelevant... no-one's getting out of here alive.

One million people die every night.

Every day when I wake up and my feet hit the floor, I say… thank you.

Thank you for giving me one more day.

I am grateful for one more day above ground.

What good can I do in the world today?

How can I grow today? How can I contribute today?

How can I be a force of positivity in the world and a force of goodness in the lives of the people I encounter today?

I look around and I see people ungrateful for today and seemingly oblivious to the fact that they're going to die, and relatively soon.

You have today… what are you going to do with it?

I spoke to another close friend last week who informed me he has just weeks left to live. He too has an aggressive brain tumour, and cancer in his lungs.

I went straight to see him to find out how I can help him to live out his life in the greatest possible comfort.

And he said to me, "The sad thing is James, there are things on my list I'm just never going to be able to do now."

Heart breaking.

He is a great man with such vitality and strength about him and I hope he proves the doctors wrong and lives strong for many more years, ticking those things off.

But it's a stark reminder that we don't want to die with anything on our list; we don't want any regrets.

Somebody once told me the worst regret you could ever have, lying on your deathbed, surround by your loved ones, when through the door walks the ghost of the person you could have been to tell you all the things they achieved, that *you* could have, but didn't.

That's the greatest regret we want to avoid.

A useful exercise to do, is to write a list of regrets you want to avoid on your deathbed.

If you don't want such a bleak thought, an alternative is to write a list of the regrets you want to avoid when you retire.

But I'm not going to ask you to do that either. I want to scale this task right back to something within reach...

Picture this… it's three years' time, you walk out of your office, and up pulls your dream car, with you in it.

Future-you leans out of the window, looking fantastic.

What would it break your heart for them to tell you, about who you could have become in that time? Is it…

- You only needed to have been working three days a week
- You could have had half the number of clients and have been making twice as much money
- Your team could have been doing all of those mundane tasks that you thought only you could do
- You could have been clearing £10k a month personally
- You could have been having 12 weeks' holiday a year with your family.
- You could have been driving this car

And when they ask you why you haven't achieved those things, what are the STORIES you're telling yourself as to why you're not there? What are your limiting beliefs? For example…

- I'm not qualified enough
- We're just a start-up business
- The clients in my town don't have much money
- My clients are mainly farmers, and they'll never pay any more
- My team don't listen to me and can't do things to my standard

YOUR TASK

1. Write down the date in three years' time, or a significant date in the future.
2. Write down your age on that date and any other life events around that time such as kids starting school or graduating, or you're turning 50.
3. Write down 5 regrets you don't want to have in three years' time.
4. What are 5 limiting beliefs you're telling yourself right now, that could possibly lead to you having those regrets?
5. Finally, what are some of the negative consequences you've experienced so far as a result of those limiting beliefs?

"You Had me Hooked When you Said - You Are Going to Die"

'I just wanted to say a huge thanks. A life changing 6 weeks for myself.

In that time, I had my second child, could only work around 15 hours per week but still was able to fully commit to this challenge and came away with a shift in mindset, the structure and ability to sell my worth and sell the services I feel my clients truly needs.

I was able to get 8 proposals (so far) agreed for total increase of over $1,200 per month. Although I might add, despite my preparation and nervousness, not one person questioned the price or the service I suggested.

Thank you, James. Your engaging and helpful sessions made for a very enjoyable process. You had me hooked when you said, "You're going to die," and only got better from there.

If you get the chance to get to Australia one day, I'd love to buy you a beer and thank you in person.'

Nathan Price | Stream Accounting

FEAR OF FAILURE

A common limiting belief is fear of failure.

I hear this a lot.

What is holding you back?

Fear.

What are you afraid of?

Failing.

But people don't ask the next and most useful question…

Who are you afraid of failing in front of?

It's not that we're afraid of failing as such, it's that we don't want to let our partner down or our parents or whoever.

A very healthy conversation to have, is to tell that person about your fear and to play it out.

Sit with them and tell them all your fears and discuss the worst possible scenario.

And every time I've ever gotten anyone to do this, they always arrive at the same point which is… it's ok. You're ok.

It normally goes something like…

So, what's your biggest fear?

My business fails.

Then what?

I'll have to get a job.

Then what?

I will probably be earning more money than I'm earning now.

Then what?

I build the confidence and my knowledge until I feel ready to go again.

Then what?

I start the business again but this time I get it right.

You see, **you only really fail if you stop.**

RECAP

Let's just stop for a moment and look at what we've just done and why.

There are two driving forces in your life… pain and pleasure.

And out of those two forces, pain is the largest motivator because your brain has one job… to keep you alive and out of harm's way.

So faced with a perceived small pain or a possible large pleasure, the perceived small pain will guide your decisions and your actions.

If I said that I can show you how to make an additional £1,000 a month for doing no more work, you might get a bit excited.

But if I said that I can show you how to stop losing £60 a month, as much as it doesn't make sense, you'd be more motivated by that, because it taps into loss and fear and pain which is what your brain is hard wired to look out for.

But when you see both roads projected forward into the future, things start to make more sense.

On one road you save £60 a month for 3 years and on the other road you make an additional £1,000 a month for 3 years. The difference in 3 years becomes vast and that intellectually and emotionally gets you to make those 2-degree changes in your direction of travel… today.

You are currently at that junction in your business and your life.

You can either go straight on, on the path you're on, or you can take a different path to hopefully greater fortunes and rewards and success.

If you associate more pain with that option because of your fear of failure, versus what you have ahead on your current path, you will keep going… even though those fears are not real.

What we've attempted to do, is explore the future pains of regret that you're facing on your current path and to look at the limiting beliefs you currently have, that are keeping you *on* that path.

We've then started to challenge the fear of taking the other path towards greater success (whatever that means for you) and it's this path that we're going to be exploring for the rest of our time together.

I know that what we've explored so far has been a little bleak. But I promise we're going to take a different direction now and there's going to be a complete gear change.

But unless you can associate enough pain with the path you're on and understand why you're on it, you will never change direction, because the perceived pain of making that change, will always be greater than your current reality.

By taking your current reality into the future and seeing how that looks and feels, is perhaps the only way to slap you off this path early enough, before you hit that actual pain in the future.

So just before we make the gear change and change in direction... just before I show you all the rewards that lie on that path for you… just before I help you to galvanise your mind and prepare your belief system for that road… and just before I give you the exact map for everything you're going to encounter on that road and how to easily navigate them… let's spend 5 minutes looking down the road you're currently on… one… last… time.

BREAKTHROUGH ACTIVITY

Pick up the notes you've just made about the regrets you want to avoid in the future, that you will likely encounter if you keep doing the limiting things you're doing.

I would like you to just sit, for 5 minutes, quietly, with your eyes closed. Imagine you're carrying on doing some of those things… still not charging enough… working even later… still dealing with those difficult clients… still not feeling valued… still taking on tasks that someone else should be doing… still not going on that holiday you would love to go on… still not driving that car you'd love to be in… still not investing time into your favourite hobby or your health, as you'd like to.

Imagine those things just getting worse and worse, this time next year, and the year after that, until eventually, the future-you pulls up in that car and tells you everything you could have been doing if only you'd made some small adjustments in your direction of travel three years ago.

Listen to those regrets and see how they make you feel.

Look at your body language. Look at your breath.

Try and really feel the pain of living with those regrets.

Imagine how you'll feel breaking up for Christmas. Imagine how you'll feel at the end of tax season. Imagine how you'll feel this time next year.

Hear the excuse you give yourself when you finally meet future-you. Write it down.

Set a timer on your phone.

Just for five minutes.

Go.

SECTION SUMMARY POSTER

On the following page is a poster I've created to help remind you of some of the concepts covered in this book, to inspire you every day.

If you want to download a printable version of this, you can get it from www.goproposal.com/untapped, as well as the other resources that accompany this book. Alternatively, you can scan this QR code, and it will take you straight there.

LIVE WITH ABUNDANCE

TO THOSE WHO HAVE EVERYTHING
MORE WILL BE GIVEN
FROM THOSE WHO HAVE NOTHING
EVERYTHING WILL BE TAKEN

THE 3 ELEMENTS OF A BREAKTHROUGH ARE
Map [Strategy]
Mindset [Story]
Mindstate [State]

STORIES PROTECT & IMPRISON
OR EMPOWER

CHANGE YOUR LIFE
CHANGE YOUR STORY

IT'S NEVER ABOUT A LACK OF RESOURCES
BUT WHETHER YOU'RE BEING
RESOURCEFUL

Nothing is happening to you
everything is happening
BECAUSE OF YOU

THE 6 HUMAN NEEDS ARE
CERTAINTY, UNCERTAINTY, SIGNIFICANCE
CONNECTION, GROWTH & CONTRIBUTION

YOU ARE GOING TO DIE

You're always making 3 decisions
What should I focus on?
What does it mean?
What am I going to do about it?

DECISIONS NOT CONDITIONS
CHANGE OUR LIFE

Success is proportional
to the amount of uncertainty
you can comfortably live with

Don't focus on what you can't control, what's missing or the past

Focus on what you can control, what you have & the present

I AM ENOUGH

GO PROPOSAL

BURN THE BOATS & MAKE A WAY

PART 4
THE BREAKTHROUGH

A CHANGE OF GEAR

That was deep and emotional and can be really tough to go through, but essential nevertheless; knowing what you want to avoid is as important as knowing what you want.

Now we're going to switch it up, but first we need to lift your energy.

Doing what we've just done will likely have put you in a low state of mind, so we need to snap you out of it.

Discovering this is the thing that stopped me from having bad days and only bad *moments* in days, because I learned how to snap myself out of it, and it starts by moving.

So just for five minutes, get your favourite music on… loud… get up, get moving, get dancing if you dare, give me some whoops, get a big old smile on your face and get ready to go again.

Warning: If you're in the car, you may need to limit those dance moves, but if you're in the office or in the middle of a coffee shop, then just go right on ahead… max level.

BREAKTHROUGH TIME

People think that breakthroughs take time; they don't.

Preparing to make a breakthrough… figuring out *how* to make a breakthrough… finding the *courage* to make a breakthrough is what can take the time, but the breakthrough itself is an instant event.

Think of it like breaking through a glass ceiling… you can't *try* to break through, you can't *half* break through, you're either breaking through or you're not.

And once you've broken through… you've broken through. There's no going back.

As Tony Robbins says, "Breakthroughs occur when your *shoulds* become *musts*."

They happen when you say…

We ***must*** *charge more or we're not going to be able to make payroll.*

We ***must*** *charge more because my health is really suffering.*

We ***need*** *to be making more money because my marriage is struggling.*

We ***must*** *charge more because I'm effectively earning minimum wage… what's the point?*

We ***must*** *charge more because I'm not seeing my kids until bedtime because I'm working so late, and I can't afford to bring in another member of staff at the right level. This needs to change and it needs to change now.*

We ***must*** *charge more because I've worked too hard for too long to be receiving this little. I'm worth so much more and there is no way I'm going to continue like this, not for another year, another month or another day.* ***It must change now.***

When you get to this point, you will do whatever it takes to make the breakthrough; you will find a way and if you can't find a way, you will make a way.

And breakthroughs are not one-off events… breakthroughs should be continual events. A breakthrough is a shedding of your shell and a moving onto the next level and the next and the next and the next.

The thought of a breakthrough can be scary for many people, but that's because they haven't been shown how to make breakthroughs effectively or been given awareness of the elements required to make the breakthrough.

"I only won this renewal because of my mindset"

'There was one client I was most concerned about re-pricing. I knew he was going to be a tough negotiator. He's a freelance salesperson and has been a client for about 2.5 years.

His fee was increasing from £115 to £226/month.

Now I'm very clear with new clients regarding who is doing the bookkeeping and if I'm doing it, I'll be charging a fee. OverSuite is forcing me to be much clearer on the scope.

This client was one I've been doing the bookkeeping for free. I added up the hours me and my team spend working on this client in a year. Having that knowledge and the mindset from James made all the difference.

I went through the proposal live. He was shocked at the increase and said he wanted to sleep on it.

No reply for 2 weeks.

He then came back, not understanding why his fee had gone up so much. So, I recorded a Loom video, to review what we discussed in the renewal meeting and in my Loom video had on the screen how many transactions he has per month.

He then came back and accepted the quote and signed an updated engagement letter. I only won this renewal because of my mindset.'

Tim Charles | Charles Accountancy

3 ELEMENTS OF A SUCCESSFUL BREAKTHROUGH

For a breakthrough to be possible, 3 elements need to be present…

The Map, the Mindset and **the Mindstate.**

But before we define these, we need to first define the breaking point, which is the point at which you breakthrough.

THE BREAKING POINT

Tony Robbins taught me that with any pursuit in life, we will hit a plateau.

Things seems to go well to start with, call it beginners' luck, but then we hit the bump… we hit a plateau. This is the breaking point.

Over the years I've come to recognise it much quicker and more clearly and feel more comfortable implementing my breakthrough strategy faster. I don't stress it, I don't question it, I just think, 'here we are again, breakthrough time, let's go...'

But breaking through isn't the only option.

When you hit the plateau - the glass ceiling - if you don't know it's there, it just manifests as frustration. You don't know why, but you're no longer progressing.

You may get a sense of frustration, but don't have the words to explain it. This can be because the part of your brain that has detected the problem, the mammalian part, does not have the concept of language like the human part of the brain does. This is why you can *feel* something isn't right but say, 'I just can't explain it.'

And because you can't explain it, it's easy to dismiss it as something less important than something you can logically explain.

But feelings are important.

Some people refer to it as 'your gut.'

In truth, it's a different part of your brain that has detected the problem and that part of the brain cannot communicate to you with words, so it will give you a feeling.

In our business, we call it a *tap*, like someone (or something) tapping you on the head.

It may be so imperceptible at the start, but if you ignore it, it will feel harder and harder.

So, as you keep hitting your head on the ceiling, feeling those taps, it's possible that you just stay stuck.

If this happens, your needs no longer get fulfilled and that's when other unwelcomed behaviours start to manifest, you stay below the line and you blame everyone and everything else for your lack of progress.

Alternatively, you keep pushing against it, but still fail to make any progress, and at some point, the pain of that ceiling will become so great that you will either have a **breakdown**, or you will **break-away**.

Your body will say enough is enough, you've not listened to my warnings, you've not read the signs, so BOOM… have a breakdown.

But in many ways, a **breakdown** is a gift because it forces a real assessment of your situation and sometimes you need to fully break down, before you garner the strength, change the direction or pick up the speed to actually break through.

Breaking away can be a gift too. Sacking it all off to go and do something else can be a legitimate strategy.

Maybe you're just not cut out to run a business. Maybe the stress is just too great and the rewards aren't enough. Maybe you just want to remove some of the entrepreneurial pressure and fulfil a role instead. And that is totally fine and can be a worthy pursuit. You just need to know in your heart of hearts that that is what you really want and that you did everything you could before making that decision.

The alternative is to **breakthrough**, and that has been my passion and purpose for almost a decade now; understanding how to achieve breakthroughs myself and also how to inspire others to do the same.

So now you know you want to make the breakthrough (which I assume you do), let's go back to those 3 elements that need to be present, for a breakthrough to be possible... **the Map, the Mindset** and **the Mindstate.**

THE MAP

Before you can get to where you want to get to, you have to know where you are now.

And as stupid as it sounds, most people don't.

Most people see themselves as either *worse* than they are or *better* than they are, but rarely *as* they are.

Accounting is beautiful for establishing where you are, because so long as there is accuracy in the numbers, the data is undeniable in pinpointing your exact location.

And once you know where you are, you need to know where you want to get to; what does life look like on the other side of the breakthrough?

Only with a start point and a clear finish, does a map become effective. If you were lost in the middle of a jungle and had no idea where you were or where you were trying to get to and I gave you a map, it would be useless.

But armed with that information and knowing exactly where you are on the map, it becomes useful.

So where does the map come from?

You have two choices.

#1 Create it yourself. Just figure it out. Chop through the jungle, clearing a space, going round and round, trying this way then that until eventually you'll find where you're going. Your experience will determine how successful this strategy will be or how long it will take.

Unfortunately, too many people burn out before they get to where they're going and I'm not sure what gets in their way.

Certainly for myself, for many years I believed I knew best and refused to ask for help.

It's like when I go to the DIY superstore (and I still do this to this day), rather than ask for help to locate something… rather than ask the people who know the store, stocked the shelves and are wearing illuminous jackets with "happy to help" emblazoned on their back… I choose to struggle and find the item for myself.

I'm not sure if that's ego or a sense of curiosity that drives that decision, but while it might be ok when looking for a widget to fix the thingy-ma-bob under the sink, it's NOT ok when looking for how to move your business to the next level so you can afford to not only feed your family but live a rich and fulfilled life.

#2 Find someone who already has it. The far easier way of getting your hands on the map is to find someone who's been on that exact journey before and who's achieving the results you want; to literally say, how are you doing that, can you give me the step-by-step guide, the blueprint, the map, the details of the path, every rock and trap to avoid, every shortcut, every snake I could slip down and every ladder I can climb, in order to get to where you are right now?

That map exists.

I will be giving you the map that has produced significant financial breakthroughs in as little as 30 days and that has set many accounting businesses on a very different path than the one they were struggling on.

One that has produced increase in revenue, improved service levels, greater impact on their client's businesses, increased profitability, improved harmony, increased morale, joy and fulfilment.

BUT… this map only works if you have the next element for a breakthrough as well… MINDSET.

THE MINDSET

Mindset is everything. But it's the hardest thing to crack.

If you show me a successful person and one who's struggling, before I even talk to them, I will know the one thing that sets them apart... MINDSET… every time.

In terms of ratios, successful people will work in favour of Mindset 80:20 in terms of Mindset:Map. That's the level of internal work this is going to require.

When you're stuck, the question to ask is not, "How do I make this breakthrough" but, "Who do I need to become, to make this breakthrough?"

As I said at the start, the thinking that has gotten you to where you are, will not get you to where you want to be; it just can't, otherwise you'd already be there.

Every breakthrough you've ever made or will make in the future, starts with a change in your thinking first.

When you know that, life becomes easier, and progression becomes possible.

But few people want to accept this. They would much rather blame their lack of progress on some external factor rather than consider the possibility of it being an internal one.

I believe you have everything you need already, to make far more progress than you can imagine.

You just need to take the brakes off in your mind...

You just need to remove conflicting thoughts and uncouple yourself from limiting beliefs and you'd be amazed at how far that will take you.

But those brakes are normally firmly locked on and the pressure is constantly being applied by the voice in your head. And here's the kicker; that voice… the one that sounds like you and talks to you all the time… isn't actually you.

You don't need to talk to **you**, in order to know what you know; you just know.

That voice is the voice of your parents, the voice of your teachers, the voice of your ex, the voice of the news, the voice of that bully or of an ex-boss.

And the really annoying thing, is that the voice does both sides of the argument while you're sat there listening.

Those voices are telling you a story. They provide you with a constant narrative, internalising the external world. But know this… those voices are afraid of change, and they will provide you with whatever story you need to hear, in order to keep things as they are and to keep you stuck.

If the voices in your head were two people in your car, jabbering away, you'd pull over immediately and boot them both out.

I need more money.

Where are you going to get more money from?

I'm going to have to increase my fees.

Who'd pay you more?

Any of my clients would. I really do a good job.

Yeah, but you're not qualified enough. You're not big enough. You don't have the skills others have.

But I could just increase my fees by a bit.

What good will that do other than annoy the client?

But I really want that holiday for my family.

But what if you lose that client? What if you lose all your clients? Then you won't be worried about a holiday, you'll be worried about keeping a roof over your head. Keep it as it is for these clients and just charge the next ones more.

OK, I'll do that.

Why? You're not making enough from the ones you have. You'd be better off getting a job.

OK, I'll do that.

But who'd employ you?

OK I'll keep going.

Why? Why don't you just give in now?

And round and round it goes. Incessant. Making no sense. Arguing one way then the other. Telling you whatever story they need to, to keep you safe, or in other words… stuck.

If you want to change your life, you have to change your story. You have to change your mindset.

You have to first become conscious of the story you're telling yourself and have the awareness to know whether it's one which is serving you, or whether it's a bullshit story that you need to change.

I have a friend, who, throughout the pandemic, put on a lot of weight. Now I'm not judging; it's just a fact and it came up in conversation.

When I asked him about his… size increase… he said it was because the gyms had closed.

That was the story he'd chosen to tell himself.

It had nothing to do with the fact that he'd been eating a lot more, drinking more alcohol, not getting out walking and not watching exercise videos on YouTube.

As they say, excuses sound best to those making them, but it was that below-the-line excuse, that was keeping him stuck, because it protected him from the truth; the truth being that he was disconnected from friends, depressed, had turned to food and drink for comfort and had become lazy and unmotivated.

If you want to change your life, you have to change your story. You have to change your mindset.

But had he had that level of self-awareness; that level of honesty, as painful as it was, he could have started to turn his situation around.

Is **your** story true? Is it serving you? Does it need to change?

Is the real reason those clients won't pay you more, REALLY because you're a small firm, not as qualified as the others, a start-up, a rural practice, because you only work with construction clients, because the competitors are cheaper, because the software makes it easier in the eyes of the client, because you like them, because their kid goes to your kid's school, because they can't afford it, because they'll leave if you increase their fees, because they've been a loyal client in the past, because they're no bother?

Is any of that story really true? Does any of it serve you? Does any of it serve the client or your team? Does it need to change?

A DISEMPOWERING STORY

A few years ago, our house was broken into by a gang of lads while we were asleep.

My wife was on a night shift as a nurse at the time, so it was just me and two young children.

The first sign I knew of the situation was the sound of my Land Rover being started on the drive.

I jumped up and banged on the window and they all ran away, unable to start the car. I went straight into the children's bedroom to make sure everyone was OK and as I did, I turned the landing light on and tripped the fuse, plunging the entire house into darkness.

I immediately panicked, not knowing if there was anyone else still in the now darkened house and so I called the police.

I waited upstairs on guard until the police came.

It turned out they'd broken in through the patio doors at the back of the house and they stole the iPad, a camera, house keys and car keys.

My wife came home right away, and I told her the story of what had happened…

OMG Bekki, I couldn't believe it.

A gang of lads broke into OUR home.

They were walking around OUR house.

We were asleep in our beds.

I was alone with the kids, and anything could have happened to them.

We were in total darkness, it was horrible.

They have the house keys so could come back at any time.

They tried to steal the car and have the keys for that too.

They took the iPad, the camera with ALL our photos on and loads of other stuff.

Just imagine if they came upstairs.

Anything could have happened… anything!!!

That was the story because that's what happened.

Look at what I've done… I've totally indulged the story and made it as bad as it could sound. Not only that, but I've also elaborated on what *could* have happened. I wasn't even content with the actual event, I fabricated future problems too… just imagine!!!

And we tell stories like this because it makes us feel significant in our tragedy.

I must've told this story to 20 people and each time it got worse and worse. I even had family and friends ringing me to see if I was ok and they would add their dramas to my story… *well you'll never guess what happened on the next street over to you...*

I then wove those stories into mine as additional dramas that could have happened as well.

Then I stopped myself and thought what am I doing?

How is this helping me?

Let me tell a different story of the same event, which was…

We were broken into because I hadn't put a side gate on, and the patio door lock was dodgy.

They took the keys, but we changed the locks immediately for more secure ones.

They didn't steal the Land Rover because it's a pig to start.

Everything else they took, we claimed back on our insurance.

The photos were all backed up to the cloud.

No harm came to us and if they had have come upstairs, I'm a second dan blackbelt in combat ju-jitsu so we would have all been alright.

It wasn't an ideal situation, but our house is now more secure and we're safer because of it.

No real harm done.

Can you see how I can tell two totally different stories about the exact same event? One empowers me and allows me to move on, while the other makes me the victim and keeps me stuck, addicted to the drama of the event and significance it gave me.

I no longer indulge in stories, and I certainly don't breathe energy into them and extend their life beyond what they deserve.

I'm too busy moving forward and building my future to be dragged down with made up dramas of the past.

I tell my kids not to talk about their problems to other people because half the people they'll tell won't care and the other half are glad they've got them. And the only people that will care, are their other loser mates, so just stop talking about them.

(My 101-parenting handbook is coming out next, btw.)

THE STORIES IN FIRMS

The stories that get told in accountancy firms, go something like…

I'm sick of this client. They don't pay us enough; they don't pay us on time, and they don't value what we do anyway.

They're always asking for more from us, but they never want to pay for it.

We've talked to them about monthly management accounts, but they don't want them, even though they need them.

They never hand their data in on time and if they do, it's always incomplete and in the wrong format.

I dread them ringing us. We just need to get rid of them and find better clients.

That story gets told to your staff and your staff believe it and even breathe life into it. They add to it and indulge it and then when the phone rings and it's that same client, it triggers the worst possible mindset because they recall the story and the feeling before they even answer the phone.

How do you think that interaction goes? Do you think the situation improves or gets worse?

They answer the phone in a rude way or send curt email responses which angers the client and exacerbates the situation.

And all because of the story they're telling, that may have elements of truth, but it is ultimately imprisoning them. And even if they were to find a 'better' client, the story would just repeat and will continue to play out forevermore; continuing to imprison, rather than empower.

But there is a different story; it's just not one that they want to tell themselves. The story they don't want to tell themselves is...

***We've** created a monster of a client here.*

***We** let them choose what they thought they wanted, rather than tell them what they really needed.*

***We** never charged them enough in the first place, we never set up an automated monthly payment with them and we never communicated the full value of what we do for them.*

***We** let those initial meetings overrun by half an hour, thereby training them not to value our time.*

*Whilst there's more we can do and more they want, **we** never sell it in the right way or have the mechanism to get them to sign up for it at the right price.*

***We** just don't know how to charge properly.*

***We** failed to train them in how to become a great client and have never corrected their bad behaviour.*

***We** should have sorted this out before now and if they truly are a bad client, we should have either had a more thorough vetting process to have spotted it up font or recognised it before now and had a conversation with them.*

***We've** created this situation and **we've** allowed it to persist.*

*This is on **us**. Let's do everything we can to make this client great and if it's too late, let's put an end to it and ensure it never happens again.*

One story imprisons and one empowers.

At the end of the last section, I asked you to write down the STORY you're telling yourself, as to why you're not further ahead.

BREAKTHROUGH ACTIVITY

Pull out that story, read it and ask yourself...

1. Am I telling myself this story to protect myself?
2. Is this story imprisoning me?
3. Is this story empowering me?
4. Is this story even true?
5. Then… with courage… write a better story.

"This year I stood strong"

'Another small monetary win (£22pm increase), but huge mindset win today. A client has just renewed - she always asks for a discount, and I usually cave and give her a £5/10 discount on renewal each year (one of my smaller monthly fees), but this year I stood strong - she asked as usual and this year I replied with: "I don't blame you for asking, but we can't move on the fees, we can't provide the level of service we would be proud of if we reduce. And she's signed no further questions.'

Cheryl Sharp | Pink Pig Financials

THE MINDSTATE

The final element required for a breakthrough is your state of mind, which we'll call Mindstate (mainly so my three words aliterate - Map, Mindset and Mindstate 😆.)

Whereas mindSET is quite fixed and takes real work to unravel, unpick and rewire with new sets of beliefs, your mindSTATE is in constant flux.

You can feel very different from one moment to the next, one day to the next.

One of the keys to maintaining a great mindstate, is not necessarily about getting yourself super fired up and mega motivated every day.

It's about blocking out the negativity which can take you into a slump. Your natural, default mindstate is good and healthy; it's the negativity that drags it down.

The news, the media and social media can do this, but that's easy to block out; just turn it off. Seriously… just turn it off. I haven't watched or listened to the news for over ten years; I don't need to.

News corporations are very aware of the reptilian part of your brain and will do everything they can to tap into your fear receptors. They have no interest in telling you anything positive. Fear keeps you hooked. Covid was the best thing that could have happened for the news outlets and there was no way they were going to let the hype surrounding it diminish.

And while ever you're consuming fear inducing story after fear inducing story, your brain's protective receptors are on high alert and start looking for danger in everything.

If, throughout the pandemic, you constantly consumed every news update, it's very easy to plunge into a mindstate of total scarcity, believing everyone's going to die, no-one has any money and the world's going to crumble.

But the world didn't crumble. It shook, but it didn't crumble.

House prices are sky high.

Amazon are doing $1.4bn a day.

I have friends in businesses across a wide range of sectors and they have never grown faster.

I'm not saying that you shouldn't be aware of what's going on in the world. But I'm just saying you don't need to consume every news update, because if you do, you have very little chance of preserving your mindstate and using your energy to propel yourself, your business and your life forward.

Choose where you get your information from; choose when.

Guard your mind like your life depends on it and don't just turn on a tap of negativity to pour in, otherwise you have no chance; literally zero chance of progression.

Another main factor that seriously affects your mindstate is the people you spend the most time with. Doing an audit of these people can be hugely valuable in giving you the best chance of maintaining a healthy mindstate for most of the time.

BREAKTHROUGH ACTIVITY

1. Make a list of the people who you spend the most time with. Out of those people, who…
   - Lights you up and gives you energy?
   - Brings you down and steals your energy?
2. Out of the people who **bring you down**, which of those people need to be **removed** from your life (seems harsh, but there are almost 8 billion people on the planet to choose from. How badly do you want this?) and which of those people need to be **managed**?
3. Of those that need to be managed, decide how often you want to have them in your life and on what terms, to best suit that relationship.
4. And of those who need to be removed, call them, thank them for their friendship, wish them well, but ultimately explain that you never want to see or speak to them again. You're welcome. NEXT!!! (8 billion, remember!!!)

I give you that task with a slight tongue in cheek, but I must confess, making that call, and I have made that call several times in my life, is probably the single activity that will propel your life forward the most.

But again, we construct stories about why we must maintain certain friendships, and it's the story, not the friendship that is holding you back, and YOU'RE in control of the story.

Is the story the truth? Does it imprison you? Does it empower you? Is there a better story that serves you?

Bottom line on this… be very mindful of the people you have around you, especially the ones you spend the most time with. You are the average of those five people.

TIPS TO MAINTAIN A POSITIVE MINDSTATE

If you can have a positive mindstate more than a negative one, then you stand a chance. Here are some top tips I've developed to maintain the mindstate you to need to keep moving forward.

1. Don't press snooze. When the alarm goes off, countdown from 5 and get up. This '5 Second Rule' by Mel Robbins is well known from her book of the same name. As she says, you don't want to fail on your first promise to yourself of the day.
2. When your feet first hit the floor, say THANK…YOU. You're above ground. You're not one of the million people who died last night, you're off to a great start.
3. Don't check your phone for the first 30 minutes of the day.
4. Start the day with some water, a stretch and a walk.
5. Try to exercise in the day.
6. Watch one motivational video on YouTube each day.
7. Sit quiet for 5 minutes each day.
8. If you feel down or angry, focus on that which you're grateful for. Write a list.
9. If you feel mega down, skip round the garden with a big smile on your face. It's impossible to be down while skipping. At least move your body; your emotion is very closely connected to motion.
10. If something goes wrong in the day, ask yourself… where is the gift in this?

11. Do something good for someone who can never repay you and try not to get found out about it. It could be as simple as buying someone a coffee in the queue behind you.
12. Seek to learn something every day.
13. Speak to a friend each day who lifts you up or who you lift up.
14. Smile. You won't run out of them.
15. When people ask you how you're doing, don't say, "Not bad." You shouldn't measure how good you are by how 'not bad' you are. You're alive in the greatest time in human history, with your amazing body and your wonderful brain, and that should be enough to reply with, "I'm outstanding thank you, how are you?"

TIME TO MOVE

The word motivation come from the Latin 'motivus', which means to move.

Many people wait until they feel motivated before they start something, but you can't; you just have to move.

And you don't even have to move by much.

You may not feel like repricing your entire client base today, that's fine, maybe you just need to reprice one.

And if repricing them seems too daunting, maybe just email them and ask if you could book a meeting in with them. There's nothing like a date in the diary to inspire action.

But if emailing them seems too daunting, maybe just clear your inbox.

And if clearing your inbox seems too much, maybe clear your desk, wash that cup, empty the bin, anything!!!

You just need to move.

And if you're not moving, maybe you've not set the bar low enough.

But there's only one force in your life that makes something move; one power. And without harnessing that power, you will stay stuck forever.

UNTAPPED by JAMES ASHFORD

THE POWER OF DECISIONS

It's the decisions you make that move you forward.

Sometimes people are so afraid of making the wrong decision, they end up making no decision.

Sometimes people spend so long making a decision, that even if it proves to be the wrong one, they stick with it, because they've invested so much time making it.

The ultimate thing to know around making decisions is that you can always decide again; you can always make another decision.

When an airplane is sitting on the runway, the pilot doesn't spend hours and hours figuring out the precise moment by moment series of decisions she'll have to make between here and arriving at the destination, such as the nuances of the map, the curvature of the earth, every other flying object in the sky at that time, the wind speed, the wind direction.

She gets to the start of the runway, revs the engine up to full speed, flies *into* the wind, gets in the air, points it in roughly the right direction and makes many decisions before she arrives at the destination.

And know this, a plane will use the majority of its fuel just to get into the air; more than it uses for the rest of the journey.

I meet some people and they're stressing about the journey and they're not even on the runway yet; hell, they're not even in the plane!!!

The ultimate thing to know around making decisions is that you can always decide again; you can always make another decision.

There is no way you can possibly know every part of the journey at the start of it; you don't have to figure out every decision along the way.

You just need to know the first one, and then make it, but most people don't even identify what the first step actually is and wonder why they're making no progress.

Start and fix it as you go.

YOU ARE ALWAYS MAKING THREE DECISIONS

Whatever's going on in the world; whatever you're in control of, or not, you're always making three decisions...

1. What am I going to focus on?
2. What does it mean?
3. What am I going to do about it?

As Tony Robbins says, '"it's your decisions, not your conditions that determine your level of success," and these three factors are at play in whatever decision you make or fail to make.

WHAT SHOULD I FOCUS ON?

Whatever you focus on, you're going to get more of.

If you focus on the fact that this client is a pain in the backside, always late, never grateful, doesn't value you and doesn't pay enough... guess what... whatever they do will only serve to reinforce this position in your mind. You have a deep desire to want to be right, so you will actively focus on aspects of this client's behaviour that reinforce your thinking of them.

But what if there are elements of this client that could make them a star? What if there's one aspect that could turn them into your number one, diamond client of all time?

Are you prepared to totally dismiss that out of a desire to be right, or would you entertain it? Would you be prepared to challenge your current thinking, your current story about that client and see them through a new lens?

The difficulty, as we discussed earlier, is when your story about this client merges with another member of your team's story, then nothing they will ever do will change how you perceive them, and you'll dismiss them out of hand.

But what if they *were* your number one, dream client of all time?

I was the pain in the backside client for my previous accountant, always late, never grateful, never valued what they did and didn't pay them enough.

Do you think they were glad to see me go? You bet!

Yet for my next accountant, I invested over a quarter of a million pounds with them over a 5-year period and WAS in fact their number one, diamond client of all time.

I was the same person.

How many clients do you have with this potential for you?

And what's preventing them from reaching that potential? Is it them, or is it what you're choosing to focus on about them?

And either way, do you know which option gives you the greatest chance of success?... believing that this is down to you and your focus, not them. Why? Because it's the thing you're in control of and it gives you the best odds of success.

Just look at the odds.

Picture a pain in the backside client in your mind and ask yourself, is the reason this isn't a wonderful, diamond client for us, down to them, or is it what you're choosing to focus on?

A. If you say it's down to them, and **it is**, you lose and so do they. And you may continue to lose if you don't do anything about it.
B. If you say it's down to them, and it turns out **not to be** (like in my case), you lose, and they go on to win. But worse than that, you continue to lose with every other potential client like them.
C. If you say it's down to your focus, and **it is**, you win, because they become a dream client, and they win too.
D. If you say it's down to your focus, and **it isn't**, at least now you know and you can part company, so you win, and they may go onto win or lose.

If you were a betting person, you have to agree that C and D have the best odds of you winning.

So why do we continue to blame the client, focus on what's bad about them and never do anything about it? Because we like to be right.

If you focus on the parts that are wrong with a client, you will start to see only the parts that are wrong.

If you focus on all the bad clients you have, you will start to see all your clients as bad.

And if you don't believe me… do this… look around the room now and only focus on the things that are red. GO!

Isn't it amazing how you were able to block everything else out and only see what's red?

But what's really interesting, is that you so desperately wanted to succeed in this task, that you saw things which were brown or purple or dusky pink and, in your mind, you made them red and counted those too… because you wanted to succeed in the task… you wanted to be right.

When you focus on only the bad in a client, not only do you fail to see the good, but you will be turning good things into bad through a desire to be right.

And most people prefer to be right, rather than happy.

Think about that for a moment.

We need to switch this lens through which we focus.

Now take that same PITA client and ask yourself…

- What did I once love about this client?
- Where's the opportunity with this client?
- What do they do right?
- How are we making them worse than they could be?
- How could we serve this client to the best of our ability?
- Where are we failing to communicate the full value of what we do?

THE QUALITY OF YOUR FOCUS

What you choose to focus on is up to you, and depending on what gets your focus, will determine the quality of your life.

Are you focussing on things you can control or things you can't?

Are you focussing on things that you have or what's missing?

Are you focussing on the present and future in a positive sense or are you focussing on the past and future in a negative sense?

If you predominantly focus on what you *can* control, what you have, the present and future in a positive light, that's going to move you forward.

If you focus on what you can't control, what's missing, the past (all the mistakes you've ever made) and the future in a negative light (everything that's likely to go wrong in the future), that's going to keep you stuck and in pain.

A PERSONAL EXAMPLE

In February 2020, the Covid Pandemic hit. No-one had ever experienced anything like this before, and as a business owner, panic set in.

I started to plan for the worst and hope for the best.

I immediately contacted my accountant and started scenario planning. What if we lost 25% of our customers? What if we lost 50%?

How would this affect our team? How would it affect my personal income? What knock-on effects would that have?

This was actually a very positive process to go through and kept us in a good mindstate, while the world was panicking. And it was only down to the quality and accuracy of data we already had in the system that facilitated this.

We made a few changes such as giving away positive video courses for our members, dialling down our marketing and supporting our customers in whatever ways we could.

You will remember that period yourself. Everyone just went above and beyond and did what needed to be done.

Thankfully, we weren't hit at all, and even remained very relevant and grew throughout it all.

Then May came and I got an email from a customer, which simply said... 'Have you seen this?'

It was an announcement made by our number one competitor, that they had done a tie-up with the ACCA.

Up until that point, the way GoProposal worked, was that customers would copy and paste the different components of their engagement letter, provided by their professional body, into the system, such as the different scopes, services schedules, terms and conditions etc...

Then as a proposal was produced, depending on the parameters entered into the system, such as start date, year-end, services, service level, client details etc... GoProposal would instantly construct the engagement letter required for that client in real-time, while they were still sat with you in the meeting.

It worked like a dream and there's no other system that does it that fast, that accurately or in a way that can be used by everyone on their team.

But what this tie-up effectively meant, was that for all ACCA members, if you wanted the engagement letter from them, that WE needed a copy of in our system, you now had to go through our competitor.

This was a blow as around 20% of our members belonged to the ACCA.

I went into panic mode.

Why have the ACCA done this?

How could they?

Is it legal?

Why didn't I think to do that?

How many clients could we lose?

Will we ever be able to get ACCA members in the future?

How much has our market been reduced?

What if they do this with all professional bodies?

What would that mean for our future?

My head was spinning. I was focussing on things I couldn't control, things that were missing, kicking myself for what we'd not done in the past and panicking about how the future was going to play out.

I was stuck and in pain… for about an hour.

Then I started to ask myself, "Where is the gift?"

This is a great question to ask in order to break the cycle of negative thinking.

You see, your focus is controlled by the questions you ask. If you want to switch your focus, ask better questions. It's really that simple.

So I started to ask myself…

Could we create our own engagement letters?

How good are the ones that accountants and bookkeepers get from their professional bodies anyway?

How long do they take to personalise?

Do accountancy firms even know how to personalise them?

Are they fit for purpose?

Who wrote them initially?

Who are the best people at writing them?

Would they write them for us?

How much time would this save our members from copying and pasting them into our system?

Is there an opportunity to do something so much better here, than has ever existed before?

How often are they updated? How long does that process take?

Do firms have compliance departments managing this? Are they even resourced to keep on top of this?

Those questions completely shifted my thinking and got me focusing on things I could control, what I had, the present and an exciting vision of the future.

Within 48 hours I had tracked down the leading authority on engagement letters in the UK. She had, in fact, written the original engagement letters for the ACCA and other professional bodies.

I got her on the phone to better understand the situation.

It turns out that some professional bodies aren't able to invest in the upkeep of the engagement letters they provide to their members, so firms have to use outdated, insufficient documents.

On top of this, firms are given a bunch of Word documents initially, which THEY have to construct into a suite of legally binding documents that perfectly reflect the firm's circumstances.

If they were to get anything wrong or to choose this paragraph instead of that one, or even get the footer information wrong, the whole document could be void, leaving the firm and their client exposed to risks.

These documents were overly wordy and filled with legalese that few people understand.

They are rarely updated and if they are, the firm then has to understand how the changes affect them and then implement those changes which, as you can imagine, rarely happens.

And for entities, such as charities and not for profit organisations, the complexity was so onerous, that a firm would need over 500 different engagement letters and be expected to perfectly pick the precise one for the circumstances of that client.

It's just not possible for a firm without a heavily manned, full-time compliance department to succeed in this and protect themselves and their clients.

My research led me to conclude that the very thing we thought we'd lost, was in fact a huge gift and an opportunity to do something so much better.

We assembled a team and set out a clear brief. The engagement letters had to...

A. Be the most robust they could in giving the firm and their clients the most protection they could.
B. Be written in clear English, for everyone to easily understand.
C. Meet the highest standards of every professional body out there (in the UK initially.)
D. Generate a full library of engagement letters within a few minutes and require no legal or contractual knowledge on the part of the firm.
E. Have all of the legislative, legal, compliance and contractual expertise built into the system and should only require simple, known inputs from the firm.
F. Be constantly updated as legislations and regulations change.
G. Automatically pull through all the key dates attached to every service
H. Enable firms to make changes if they needed to.

I. The final production of the engagement letter should be able to be completed in front of a client, in under 5 minutes, by a 10-year-old, with no more than 20 minutes training, even for the most complex of organisations, such as a charity. (This was a parameter we set, and it was proven by my ten-year-old daughter, Scarlett.)

The entire project took 5 months to complete.

It was intense and the outcome far exceeded both ours and our customer's expectations.

The product was named OverSuite, and not only did it prevent the loss of any of our clients, but it has also become a profit generating feature in its own right and will soon be a stand-alone product.

It is now widely recognised as the leading engagement letter product on the market and some of the major professional bodies are wanting to replace their own templates with it.

Engagement Letters are one of those things that firms think is a box ticking exercise. We have an engagement letter… tick. But they don't know how robust it is and if it ever got brought out of the drawer, how protective it would be.

There are few people who know of all the possible risks that could cost you money, cost you time, cost your sanity or cost you your business.

We've had the privilege of working with these people who have layered their expertise through the documentation to afford even the smallest of firms, the same level of protection that the top firms have.

So, when I read stories like this from Hannah Adams, it lights me up:

"We acquired a client in November 2020, and they signed up using the GoProposal engagement letters and proposals straight away. We drafted the accounts and sent them over for approval. They then went radio silent.

Fast forward to late 2021 and our bill remained unpaid (we don't submit unless payment is received for the work we've done), and they began to argue that they hadn't instructed us and that they didn't know why we were doing their accounts - despite being added to their Xero account and being provided with their accounts information!

The relationship had broken down and the only recourse we had was to take them to the courts to get our money. They ended up with a CCJ.

Fast forward to last week and they got back in touch. They apologised, and had someone looking over the documentation to check where they legally stand.

Thanks to the engagement letters we had from GoProposal, it was confirmed they didn't have a leg to stand on. Had we not had these documents in place I think we could have kissed goodbye to our fee. They are now paying our fees.

If you're ever questioning the fees you pay to GoProposal, just think about how much an unpaid fee can impact your business. For us our GP fee (and subsequent OverSuite fee) is something I would never cut from our business, it's invaluable."

- **Hannah Adams**

So, what's my point? It's not your conditions that determine your success, but your decisions.

We turned a threatening situation into a tremendous opportunity for ourselves and our customers, simply by shifting our focus.

We shifted that focus by asking better questions.

We focused on what we could control, what we had, the gift in the situation, the present and a brighter future.

We all face the same winds… winds of challenge, winds of the economy, winds of competitors, winds of a pandemic, winds of change, winds of loss, winds of opportunity… we all face the same winds.

But it's not the winds that determine where you'll end up in 3 months, 12 months, 36 months' time… but how you set your sail.

ARE YOU ENOUGH?

Whatever you focus on, you're going to get more of.

The questions you ask yourself control your focus.

Earlier on, I asked you to consider a very disempowering question, which is at the root cause of all your fears… "Am I enough?"

And I asked you to consider some of the limiting beliefs that you associate with that question.

That question controls your focus in a negative way and invariably leads to answers that are keeping you stuck and in pain.

I want to show you how you can completely shift your focus, with the addition of just one word that makes it a better question…

HOW am I enough?

BREAKTHROUGH ACTIVITY

Previously, I asked you to write down 5 limiting beliefs, which if you continued to believe, would hold you back.

1. I want you to find those limiting beliefs and put a single line through each of them.
2. I now want you to write five empowering beliefs, that you have about yourself, that confirm HOW you are enough.

These are five beliefs that have the power to propel you forward.

They have to be true. You're a smart person. You can't start making false affirmations to yourself and expect your brain to just believe them because you've chanted them multiple times.

But a true empowering belief could be…

- I care so deeply that I will do whatever it takes to serve our clients to the highest possible levels.
- I have enough ability to adapt my knowledge to positively impact our clients.
- I am worth so much more and I am prepared to charge what I'm worth.

Once you've identified your five empowering beliefs, I want you to pin them up on your fridge or bathroom mirror. I want them to be somewhere you're going to read them every day. I need you to believe these to your core.

As you write them, I just want to give you a word of warning about the phrase 'I am' or 'we are'.

'I am' or 'we are', are very powerful phrases.

You must always be very guarded about what follows 'I am' or 'we are.'

'We are a small firm' is not as empowering as 'we are a nimble firm.'

'I am only qualified in X' is not as empowering as 'I am hugely proud to be qualified in X.'

'I am only a bookkeeper' is not as empowering as 'I am the most diligent bookkeeper you will ever meet who will unlock accurate data fast, so you can make more informed decisions about your business.'

WHAT DOES IT MEAN?

Remember… there are three things you're always in control of; three questions you're always asking… '**what should I focus on?**' is the first… '**what does it mean**?' is the second.

The meaning you give to something will determine the level of emotion you ascribe to it.

When anything is happening or whenever you're doing something, you have a narrative going on in your mind about that thing.

One thing I'm very good at is taking control of that narrative.

For example, I'm the only person in our house who actually enjoys washing the pots or emptying the dishwasher and it comes down to the narrative I have in my head.

The narrative determines the meaning, and the meaning changes my emotion and ultimately my mindstate.

When most people wash pots, in their head, I imagine it runs something like… *Why should I have to do this? What else could I be doing? Why is it always me? Who else should be doing this? I'm sick of this. I've just chipped my bloody nail. Urgh, what's that gunk in the bottom of the sink? Who hasn't scraped their plate properly?*

In my head, my narrative runs something like… *Aren't I lucky to have a house and a family to clean up after? Let's get these pots as clean as possible for me to serve their next meal on. Aren't I blessed to have hot running water?*

The task is the task. It's the same for both of us. The only difference is that I choose to take control of my emotions by controlling the narrative.

If I ever drop anything or spill something, my instant reaction is to laugh. I've learned to do this. Why?

Because I've concluded that I have to clean it up anyway, so I'm either going to do that whilst smiling or do it whilst being annoyed. Either way it needs to be done, but in one situation I'm controlling my emotion and in the other, the spilled item is controlling it.

Picture this if you will. I want you to think back to one of your first clients. I want it to be the client that started paying you a large fee. Out loud, make the sound that described how you felt when that client signed up.

[MAKE SOUND NOW] and no, I don't care if you're still in that coffee shop.

Now, picture that same client, who is likely still paying you the same fee, but who you're probably doing more work for. When you see their number show up on your phone, how do you feel now?

[MAKE SOUND NOW]

Now I imagine that the first noise you made sounded something like 'WAHOO,' and the second noise sound something like 'Urrgghhhhhhh!'

The first was filled with jubilation and the second filled with trepidation.

So, what's changed? It's the same client.

I imagine what's changed is the meaning you've ascribed to that client.

When they first signed up it meant growth and excitement and opportunity and more money.

Now when they call it means that they're taking your time, preventing you from doing other things and a feeling of being undervalued.

Since that client first signed up, perhaps you've developed new strategies for how to deal with clients. Perhaps now they would pay you much more and as they ask for more, you charge more. Perhaps they no longer deal with you directly but deal with a team member instead.

But rather than change the strategy with this client and have that courageous conversation, you've just changed the story instead, to justify how they're making you feel.

That story gives the situation meaning, the meaning controls your emotion and that emotion effects your levels of motivation to do anything about it.

What if I said you have to wake up at 4:30 in the morning. How would that make you feel? Not very good perhaps and why? Because of the story you associate to that... *that's way too early, I'll be tired all day, what's the point?*

But if I said you have to wake up a 4:30am in the morning because there's a car pulling up to take you to the airport, because you're going on holiday, how would that make you feel? Excited? Energised? Happy? Motivated?

What's different? It's the same time. You just have a different meaning associated to it, which changes your emotions, your mindstate and ultimately your level of motivation.

And your level of motivation is critical.

As I said, the word 'motivation' comes from the Latin 'motivus', which means 'to move.'

And this takes us into the final phase of what we can control... **What should I focus on?** ... **What does it mean?** ... and... **What am I going to do about it?**

WHAT AM I GOING TO DO ABOUT IT?

To do something, requires action. But if you are in a terrible state of mind because of the meaning you've ascribed to that thing, you will not move yourself into taking action and will therefore stay stuck.

It's time to move.

To move forward, we must know where we are, where we're going and how to get there. We must have the right mindset and be in the right state of mind.

You have to feel motivated in order to take action and if you don't feel like you can make a move at that point, it's either because you're focusing on the wrong thing, you're not giving it the right meaning and are therefore in totally the wrong mindstate or you believe there is something preventing you from being able to move.

When we feel there is something preventing us from moving forward, we typically blame a lack of resources. Those resources include a lack of...

- Money
- Time
- People
- Knowledge
- Energy
- Technology

But the reason why we don't progress is never an issue of a lack of resources and is always an issue of resourcefulness.

It doesn't matter what you don't have, it all boils down to what you DO have and how you make the most of what's in front of you.

If you can't find a way, make a way.

If you only have a wall and you're looking for the door and there isn't one... run through the wall... like I did on Valentine's Day 2015.

VALENTINES DAY 2015

Valentine's Day 2015 fell on a Saturday.

I promised my wife I'd take her to the best restaurant in town, which happened to also be one of the smallest, called The Rum Rooms.

It was the Wednesday before Valentines and Bekki asked me if I'd booked a table yet. I told her I hadn't, so she called the restaurant instead.

I couldn't quite hear the guy's response, but I could hear him laughing quite loudly on the phone and took that to be a bad sign.

Apparently, they'd been booked up since last year, he was very sorry and suggested we tried another time.

My wife had a few choice words for me, none of which are printable here, but I reassured her that I'd sort it.

It was now the Friday, the day before and I still hadn't booked a table, so I thought I'd try the restaurant again on the off chance they'd had a cancellation.

As I expected to be the case, they hadn't, and he told me the same thing he told Bekki… they were booked up, had been since last year, so no chance, sorry.

I said to him, "Can I just ask, what is it a problem of? Is it tables, because we have a small table at home, I could bring it and we could squeeze in the corner?"

"No." He said quite sternly, clearly thinking I was crazy, "We just don't have enough space. We're a small restaurant and can only fit in so many tables upstairs."

"OK." I said, "What about downstairs?"

"That's the bar," he said, growing more impatient. "That's even smaller and for drinking only. We just don't have the room, sorry."

I thought. They had a dark courtyard out the back of the restaurant.

"What about the courtyard outside? Could we possibly fit a table out there?" I asked.

"It's dark out there," he replied.

"Ok, how could you make it lighter?" I asked.

"Well, we could put some fairy lights up, but it's February." He said, "It's freezing out there."

"OK." I said, "How could we make it warmer?"

"Well," he said, "I guess we could put some blankets out there and a fire basket for you and I suppose that would make it lighter too."

And it was in that moment that his focus changed on what was possible versus what wasn't.

I felt it shift.

"Perfect.," I said, "What time should we come for?"

"8:30pm," he said.

Bingo!!!

What was different to me versus everyone else who had called, asking for a table?

The situation was exactly the same.

The difference was that I was focused on something else; I was focused on us eating there on Valentine's Day, not whether he had a table or not. And I was resourceful.

I told my wife we had a table booked and she asked how. I thought if I tell her we're sitting outside in February, I've blown it, so I kept quiet.

When we got there, the setting was beautiful.

There was a single table in the middle of the courtyard, with a fire basket next to us, logs for the fire, candles on the table and fairy lights all around.

Some people even came out asking how we'd managed to get this?

My wife was happy.

But that's not the best part.

When we went back 3 months later, the guy recognised us and told us to come and look outside.

He'd created a purpose-built outdoor eating area, increasing the size of his restaurant by about 25%.

The next time we went back it had grown again to almost double the size.

And the time after that, it was a full outdoor events space with a bar and dining area, and I like to think that my persistence and resourcefulness is what sparked this expansion.

The thing standing in our way is not a lack of resources, but a lack of resourcefulness. You have everything you need to move forward right in front of you, right now.

In order to be resourceful, you have to be hungry.

And the story you tell yourself will either fuel your hunger or kill it off.

On top of this, you have to be **relentless,** and you have to be **unreasonable.**

"The reasonable man adapts himself to the world: the unreasonable one persists in trying to adapt the world to himself. Therefore, all progress depends on the unreasonable man."

- **George Bernard Shaw**

THE CHINESE BAMBOO PLANT

I want you to have a breakthrough and I want it to be significant and lasting.

And for this, I always take inspiration from the Chinese bamboo plant.

The Chinese bamboo plant requires daily watering and feeding in order to grow.

You have to plant the seed and water that spot, every day, for 5 years, and during that time you will see NOTHING!!!

If anyone were to see you and didn't know what you were up to, they would think you were crazy, just watering that same spot of earth for 5 years, every day, with nothing to show for it.

But then sometime in year five, the shoots break through the surface of the earth and the plant grows to 90ft tall in just 6 weeks.

The growth that comes on the other side of the breakthrough can be sudden and immense.

It's everything that's been growing within you, beneath the ground that takes the time, preparing for the breakthrough, but the breakthrough itself is an instant event.

You are ready for this breakthrough.

But what causes the breakthrough moment?

The pain.

THE PAIN IS A GIFT

Pain is a gift, because it's the pain that sparks the breakthrough.

Most of us attempt to dull the pain with either vices or the stories we tell ourselves, rather than face the pain.

But pain is a gift… like it is for the lobster.

If the lobster had pain killers of some sort, it would stay in its painful, restrictive shell and never grow.

For years I developed many techniques to dull the pain, rather than face it.

But we have to find the courage to shed the shell and grow a new one, because it was only at that moment in my life, that everything started to change for me.

But I believe there's a specific trait of accountants and bookkeepers that makes this especially difficult.

THE ACCOUNTANT'S CURSE

We talked earlier about how everyone has a need for **certainty** and a need for **uncertainty.**

Accountants and bookkeepers, *by their very nature,* that led them into this profession, tend to have a greater propensity for certainty.

However… your ability to grow, is directly proportional to the amount of UNcertainty you can comfortably live with.

If you're not prepared to shed the shell that causes you the pain, you can't grow or move forward, and there is a level of uncertainty and vulnerability that comes while the shell is off.

If you can't comfortably live with a degree of risk, of embarrassment, uncertainty or challenge, you will stay where you are and you will be unable to find a way forward.

But I believe you are incredible and capable of so much.

You will never be given a challenge you cannot break through.

And if you can't break through it yourself, you have the ability to find people who can help you.

The very chance you are alive is said to be 14 trillion to one.

There's a book by Zig Ziglar called "Born to Win."

I don't believe you were born to win; I believe you were born *because* you won.

The very fact that you are here is astounding.

The things you've been through in your life so far prove that you are unstoppable.

One of my favourite quotes of all time is from Jim Rohn, who said...

"Don't wish it were easier, wish you were better. Don't wish for fewer problems, wish for more skills. Don't wish for less challenge, wish for more wisdom."

- **Jim Rohn**

TALKING A GOOD FIGHT

There are lots of people who say they want to be successful, but there are far fewer people who take the necessary actions to get there.

Over the years I've encountered many accounting businesses through their interaction with GoProposal and I can split them into two camps.

Those who say...

I'm going to do X and we'll see what happens.

And those who say...

I'm going to do X and we'll make it happen.

Which of those two people do you believe will be successful?

The key here is that we can't half break through; we can't dabble. We have to be fully committed to fully breaking through.

We have to burn the boats.

BURN THE BOATS

Hernando Cortez came from Spain and had gone in search for treasure in South America.

His wife had been kidnapped during this conquest and was taken hostage on an island where all the treasure was said to be held.

But the problem he faced was that the opposing army was far larger than his.

So, when they landed on the island, the first instruction he gave his men was to burn the boats.

They removed all options of retreat, so they had to become resourceful, and relentless and this ultimately led to their victory.

I always remembered this lesson and took it to heart.

My first job after university was teaching art in prisons, near where I lived.

Deep down I had a desire to setup my own business, but this paid good money and was a solid option at the time.

After the first year they explained that even though I had a master's degree, I needed a teaching qualification in order to continue working there.

I started my teaching qualification and got to the end of the first year, but I just couldn't bring myself to complete the final assignment.

I remember sitting in the kitchen with my head in my hands when my wife walked in.

She asked me what was wrong, and I explained how I was struggling with this final assignment.

She said, "The thing is James, if you just complete this and get your teaching qualification, *you'll always have something to fall back on.*"

As she left the room, her words were ringing in my head… *something to fall back on.*

I picked up all my paperwork from that year, went out into the garden, threw them into a metal bin and set them on fire.

My wife came running out shouting, "What are you doing?"

And I said, "I love you, but I don't need anything to fall back on."

After that I went on to set up my first business… and it failed.

Having nothing to fall back on, I set up my next and the next until I eventually had the breakthrough I was looking for with GoProposal, and that breakthrough changed my life and the lives of those around me.

I removed all other options and I found a way.

We only get so many laps of the sun.

You are an amazing person and I know you have everything you need to break through the challenges you're facing.

You just need the map, the mindset, the mindstate and the motivation to drive this through.

BREAKTHROUGH ACTIVITY

Your final task of this section is to identify...

- What one small task could you comfortably do right now, that would start things moving forward for you?
- What large, difficult decision could you make that would profoundly change everything for you?

Please write those down.

Now I hope you feel fired up and energised to take action.

The best advice I can give you is that while you're in this state, just **take one step towards one of your goals RIGHT NOW**. It only needs to be small one, but it's far easier to take it right now, rather than in an hour or tomorrow.

Just take one step, whether that's to email a member of your team, to book some time out in your diary for a task, buy a book or whatever.

We are now going to start taking these theories and ideas and setting them into firm, strategic actions that WILL move you forward.

I KNOW you're a good person.

I KNOW that you care deeply.

I KNOW that you work hard.

I KNOW you deserve more than you're getting now.

I KNOW that this book can help you to get what you deserve.

I KNOW it starts now.

It's time to make a way.

PART 5

PREPARE FOR SUCCESS

BE OUTCOME FOCUSSED

From this point forward, I need you to become **outcome** focussed as opposed to **task** focussed.

Very often we busy ourselves with tasks and confuse that activity with progress. But very often it's just laziness.

Now you don't like me calling you lazy because you are working flat-out for ridiculous hours. But what I mean by laziness is, 'avoiding doing the things you know you need to do, in order to move yourself and your situation forward.'

Working hard on the wrong tasks, is lazy.

I don't care about the tasks; I care about the results and so should you.

People love to ask, 'Are you busy?' And you love to tell them that you are. We wear our busyness as a badge of honour.

A far better question to ask is, 'Are you achieving the results you want to achieve in your business?'

The goal is not to complete tasks. The goal is not to be busy. The goal is to achieve results. And if you can achieve your results by 11:00 AM and spend the rest of the day in the gym or with friends or in the beer garden then great. If you can achieve your results by Wednesday and spend four days in your garden or on holiday, then fantastic.

I don't care how busy you are, I care about the results you're achieving, and you should too.

URGENCY VERSUS IMPORTANCE

I'm sure you will have seen a variation of the Eisenhower Matrix before. Along one axis is the level of urgency and along the other is the level of importance.

This creates four squares as you can see.

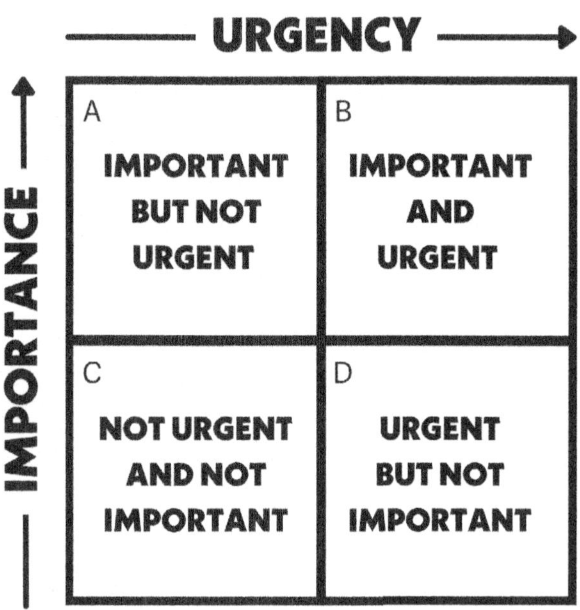

If you imagine all your tasks were split among the four squares – A, B, C & D - which one should you be spending your time in?

If you said B, I'm afraid you're wrong. The answer is A.

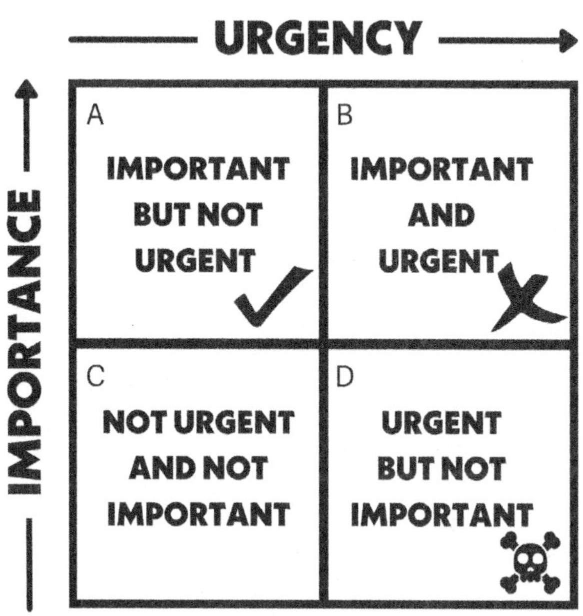

If you can focus your time on IMPORTANT BUT **NOT** URGENT tasks, you prevent them from ever becoming urgent.

Repricing your clients is IMPORTANT

However, if you don't do it soon, at some point it will become URGENT.

Pushing for your clients to give you their data to complete their tax returns early in the year is IMPORTANT but perhaps NOT URGENT.

If you leave it until the last month before the deadline, it's now IMPORTANT AND URGENT.

So, we ideally want the level of IMPORTANCE to govern our priorities, not the level of URGENCY.

That said, there will always be times when you have no choice but to deal with URGENT AND IMPORTANT tasks; an upset client on the phone, a fantastic opportunity, something hitting the fan.

The point is… we don't want to remain in that square.

The square of death that kills many businesses' progress is D… URGENT BUT NOT IMPORTANT.

And in a forever connected world, anything pinging or dinging on your phone, your watch or laptop is always deemed URGENT and pulls us into that square.

Why do you think that emails need responding to every day?

Yes, you need ensure that all client emails are responded to every day by your team or an outsourced pa, but for me, the person working ON the business, I look at my inbox once a week or I'd go out of my mind and never get anything done.

Who said you can't ignore phone calls or texts?

If I'm in the zone of getting an important piece of work over the line, like writing this book for example, I am happy to ignore calls and texts and messages… I'll just apologise later.

I'm happy for people to be annoyed with me. Are you?

And if not, what you're saying is... how you're perceived by others and how you're made to feel when you let people down, is more important than getting the shit done that's actually going to make your life better.

The image others have of you and your own feelings, are more important than progress... *that's* what you're saying.

If you were in a meeting with a client, other people wouldn't be able to get hold of you.

If you were on holiday, other people shouldn't be able to get hold of you (I hope).

I always leave my phone at home when I go on holiday, because at that moment, my family and my mental well-being is THE most important thing in the world.

It's OK to drop balls you know; there are different types of balls.

There are glass ones and rubber ones and wooden ones and plastic ones and metal ones. All you must do is not drop the glass ones. It doesn't matter about the others. They'll be ok, you can pick them up, dust them down and say sorry.

And if those balls really mind about being dropped, then they probably don't matter, because if they really matter, they won't mind that you've chosen to progress your life over replying to that email or picking up that phone call.

One of my friends is one of the most successful business owners I know. He lives an amazing lifestyle, drives a Bentley, flies first class, is always present for his three kids, has a house in the USA and UK, makes millions every year, owns scores of houses which he's paid for in cash and has millions in the stock market.

This guy is crushing it and he's always so happy and positive. He's one of my best friends on the planet and there can be weeks when I can't get hold of him… WEEKS!!! And I love that because I know he is either making HIS life, his FAMILY'S life or his CLIENT'S life better.

You also must ask yourself, when we think of IMPORTANT and URGENT… Important to who?... Urgent to who?

Is this really important in helping you to progress your life and your business or are you prioritising what is important to that client? You know… the one who never does what you ask them, refuses to take the services you recommend and always quibbles over price… that client… who's just called you and desperately needs you to complete something important… NOW!!!

Over the next 90 days I need you to become super focussed on the important activity of making more money in your business, because I know it will solve many of your problems.

If you can't get your head around what I'm sharing with you here, you just won't make it happen and you'll still be stuck working too hard for too little, chasing non-important tasks and being a busy fool.

BREAKTHROUGH ACTIVITY

My question to you is… how can you free up your time?

What can you delay, delete or delegate?

What just isn't important for you to do?

What three, recurring tasks could you get other people to do?

Sure, they might not do those tasks as well as you. You may be able to complete that task to a 90% standard and if you got your colleague to do it, it would be 75%.

But guess what? You have all these tasks on your list which you *could* complete to 90%, but because you're so busy, you're actually completing them at 0%.

You're far better off getting your colleague to complete them to 75% and then train them to get to 78% and then 83% and so on, otherwise it will always be on you to complete. Just…

- Record a quick video showing them exactly what to do
- Write out a checklist of points you would need to see achieved, if someone else were to do the task
- Put a check in place to ensure the standard you expect is met
- Hand it over and get out of the way

It really is as simple as that.

"Proves it's all in my head"

'I've done a renewal... but I feel a bit cheated as I was going for a full meeting and he popped into the office and said look I've been so busy where do I sign. It was only £123 per month extra, but that's a mulberry bag a year. Proves it's all in my head.'

Carrie Stokes | Spotlight Accounting

BECOME MILITARY MINDED

When a mission is planned in the military, they focus on the outcome.

Yes, they will have a plan as to how they will achieve that outcome, but they know that as soon as you encounter the enemy, the plan is out of the window, which is why everyone needs to be focussed on the outcome.

Mike Tyson said, "Every boxer has a plan until they get smacked in the mouth."

You must have a clear outcome in mind, because if you just focus on the tasks, the moment you get metaphorically smacked in the mouth, you'll stop.

If you were planning a military mission for example, you might have an outcome to take the enemy's base.

The plan might be….

- 4 soldiers take a vehicle
- They drive it up the hill
- They capture the first guard
- They break the perimeter of the base
- Blow the back door
- Take control of the base

But if they get to the vehicle and it's out of fuel, they don't all return home. They adapt the plan, remain focused on the outcome and do what they need to, to get there.

I see many accountancy firms set a plan to reprice 10 clients, let's say, and fail. Their plan may be...

- Identify the 10 clients that need repricing
- Find their phone numbers
- Call them and schedule an appointment
- Have a meeting where you discuss and agree their fee
- Produce a proposal (using GoProposal of course)
- Get it accepted
- Raise their fee

What happens?

You speak to your team a few weeks later to see how they got on and they've only managed to set two appointments, they've had one meeting and they still need to produce a proposal.

When you push them as to why they failed, they say they didn't have the phone number for 3 of the clients, the next 3 didn't answer their phone, the next one was on holiday, the next didn't want to have a meeting, two scheduled a meeting and they've done one.

But that wasn't the outcome.

The outcome should have been to increase the fees of 10 clients.

So, if they didn't answer the phone, they should have been called again... and again.

If you're not resourced to do that, then you should use an outsourced calling specialist.

If they still don't answer...

- Text them
- WhatsApp them
- LinkedIn message them
- Send them a personalised video
- Write them a handwritten note
- Send them a giant cookie with a message on
- Turn up at their office
- Send a choir to their office
- Ask your mum to go round with a cake she's baked

I really don't care what you do. The outcome is to increase the fees of ten clients.

If they're totally nonresponsive... send notice that you'll cease their payments and service unless they accept the fee increase.

Get resourceful. Be relentless. Find a way.

What you can't do is fail just because only 2 people answered the phone. How many times did you call? Once or one hundred times?

Did you leave a voicemail? Did you sing the voicemail? Did you pay for a cheap D-list celebrity to send them a message for £50?

I don't care what you **do**, I care about the **outcome**.

And the reason why most outcomes aren't fulfilled is because the WHY isn't set.

THE IMPORTANCE OF THE WHY

Let's go back to the military objective.

It's not enough to say that we need to capture the enemy base.

The soldiers need to know that if they don't, half of our men are going to be involved in a surprise attack in the morning and many of them will lose their lives.

It's the "why" that drives the resourcefulness and gets the outcome over the line.

It's no good saying to your team member that they need to reprice 10 clients. They need to know WHY.

It is far more compelling to say to your team... we need to reprice 10 clients this month and here's why...

- We are all working too hard and not getting enough rewards from it
- I'm working 6 days a week and I know many of you are working late each night and are massively stressed
- That's not why I setup this business
- I want to only work 4 days a week and I want you all finishing your tasks by 3pm each day
- I want to invest in team training, employ a new admin member of staff to take a lot of weight off you and I want for every time that phone rings, it's a client who massively values us
- I also want to give you all a pay-rise
- But we can't do that if we don't make more money

- I need to increase our MRR by £10k over the next 6 months
- To do that, we need to reprice all our clients and to be on track, we need to reprice ten of them this week
- Do you all understand the supreme importance of getting these ten fee reviews booked into the diary?
- Fantastic, now do whatever it takes to get those renewal meetings booked into the diary this month

Can you see the difference with that approach?

Can you see the importance of setting a very clear outcome and backing it up with a compelling reason why?

And when we do this, we need to be very mindful of our words.

Words have power.

If you say to someone, "Let's try to get these meetings booked in this month," I guarantee it won't happen.

Just like if a friend asks you to a party this weekend and you say you'll 'try' to make it. You're not going; we all know that.

But if you have a different level of conviction and say, "We must get these meetings booked in this month. Who's with me?" It will.

But even with this level of conviction and the support of a compelling reason why, most people will still fail because they are not really prepared for the enemy, as they've never been told what the enemy is.

The enemy is not your client.

But the enemy is very real, will definitely show up and it does have a name.

And if you're not prepared for it, you will fail, because it's not just trying to derail your plans… the enemy is so much worse than that.

YOUR REAL ENEMY

How can you go into battle if you don't know who or what your enemy is?

And as easy as I'm going to make it for you to make more money… fighting for what you're worth *is* a battle.

And if you're not prepared for the enemy when it arrives, you will likely fall at the first hurdle.

I first learned about this from an author called Steven Pressfield who described it in great detail in his fantastic book "The War of Art."

It's a very short, powerful book and he has others around this too, such as "Do the Work" and "Turning Pro." All great books and worth a read.

He wrote the film "The Legend of Bagger Vance" starring Will Smith.

In the book, he describes how whenever we embark on a challenge that we perceive to move our life forward, whether that's weight loss, improving our health, setting up a business, starting an artistic endeavour, writing a book, seeking a new partner, making more money… whenever we attempt to do anything to improve our lives, a force will come to try and stop us from achieving it.

And he calls that force: **Resistance.**

Your enemy in improving the finances of your business is Resistance and I have encountered it many times.

In Pressfield's books, he not only says that this force is trying to *prevent* you from achieving your goals, he says it's actually trying to *kill you.* And only when you understand the level of the force you're up against, will you begin to match it with an equal or more powerful level of effort.

Some things you need to know about Resistance are that…

- It doesn't care about you
- It's not personal
- The greater the goal you're trying to achieve, the greater the level of resistance you're going to meet
- The closer you get to your goal, the stronger the force will get
- It will use anything it can to stop you in your tracks
- It will use the voice in your head, it will lie to you, it will trick you, it will call upon your most painful past events, it doesn't care
- It can even use people around you to put doubt in your mind. And as strange as that sounds, I have experienced it, even from people who love me very dearly

Now I don't want to go too deep into this. If it interests you and you want to understand it at a deeper level, go and read "The War of Art."

For the purpose of what we're trying to achieve here, all you need to know is that you are up against a malevolent force that you will awaken the moment you try to make your life better, and it's called Resistance.

Resistance is the enemy and if you don't know it now, you will know it soon.

A COMMON FORM OF RESISTANCE

One of the first forms of Resistance you will encounter will be a lack of time.

Resistance will convince you that you don't have enough time to do the things you need to do.

It will throw everything in your path to take your time away from you and in the past, you have thought this is just how it is, or this is because that member of staff isn't skilled enough, or that client really needs to speak to me, or it's your mate's birthday party, or your phone has just stopped working, or whatever.

Now, the moment something like this happens, label it… this is Resistance showing up.

As I'm writing this book, I have people wanting to book a 15-minute call with me in my diary to chat about something.

It's just 15 minutes, right? What harm can it do?

WRONG!!! That's Resistance showing up.

And then the voice kicks in, in your head… what if they're pissed off at me, what if it's an opportunity of a lifetime, it's only 15 minutes, what harm can it do?

THAT is also Resistance showing up.

The invite and the voice are both Resistance.

I just reply with… I'm stacked for the next 2 months, when's good after that?

If it is mega important, I may say, look, I can't meet for an hour, but I can talk on the phone with you for 3 minutes right now, before I go into my next meeting if that helps?

Taking your time is one of the first tricks Resistance will use.

But know this... it's never an issue of time... it's always an issue of **prioritising** and **focus**.

Even as I write this line (and this is the absolute truth), my son is sat opposite me, trying to talk to me about buying a music pack for Beat Saber on his VR headset. I am completely ignoring him because it's just Resistance. He knows how much money he has in his bank and knows he is empowered to make his own decision around how he spends it. He doesn't need me to help him with that.

And if I didn't ignore that and the thousands of other interruptions, you wouldn't be reading this right now. The completion of this book by the end of this month is my priority.

We all roughly spend the same number of hours at work.

The only reason why someone achieves more with their time than you with yours, is their ability to prioritise and focus.

Know this… it's never an issue of time… it's always an issue of **prioritising** and **focus**.

Now Resistance has just popped it's head up and said... no it's not... it's because they are multi-millionaires and billionaires and are super talented and have teams of people around them.

Yes... but they only got to that point by working ridiculously hard on the right things, continually, for prolonged periods of time... no other reason.

And... they only did that by prioritising and being focused and constantly overcoming Resistance.

I know how good you are at prioritising and being focussed by asking you one simple question...

When do you check your emails? Is it:

A. As soon as you wake up
B. As soon as you get to work
C. At lunchtime
D. Last thing in the day
E. Last thing in the week
F. I have someone else managing my emails for me

If you answered A or B you're screwed.

If you do that, you are inviting so many unknowns into your world and because everyone else knows that's what you do, your clients and your team will change their behaviours to suit.

If you are CC'd into an email with other people on your team, are you the first to respond? If you answered yes, you are training your team to sit back and relax because they know you'll step in and sort it out.

The words "rod" and "for your own back" spring to mind.

If you want to move something forward in your business, know what your goal is for that day and start on it early, without checking emails and with no interruptions.

Tell your team that you will not be responding to anything in mornings from now on… not emails, phone calls or texts. You won't even be available for a 10 second chat.

Focus the first few hours of each day on **you**.

Now that all might sound great, but again, Resistance has just made an appearance in your head saying, "But what if someone really needs you? What if there's a problem? What if something's hit the fan that only you can clean up?"

So long as you're the first person to solve the problem, you always will be. And unknowingly, you are accidentally diminishing your team, because you are depriving them of valuable lessons and learnings for them to grow and step up.

It's like you want them to remain children and for you to remain the parent and I get it, there is some fulfilment in that. We feel wanted and useful and valued.

But you need to let go.

Empower.

Create a space for people to flourish and feel safe enough to fall.

Get them to run experiments.

Get out of their way.

Get out of your way.

Let's say you were in a super important client meeting tomorrow morning for 4 hours, that they were paying you £1,000 to help them solve some huge problems in their business and to significantly move them forward.

If you were in that meeting from 6am tomorrow, would you be checking your emails and taking phone calls, or would you give them your undivided attention and energy?

Would you try and distract yourself beforehand by just checking your emails first or would you want to show up fresh, ready to do your best work?

So why don't you afford yourself the same privilege of your undivided focus and attention each and every day?

Could you imagine where you'd be if you did?

But you've managed to convince yourself that you always need to be contacted in case of an emergency.

But when have you ever needed to be contacted in an emergency, that only you could solve, in that moment?

The answer is rarely, if ever.

Once I was called into school because my son was *feeling* sick (he hadn't been sick, he just felt sick).

I went into see him and asked him if he was ok, and he was a little bit off-colour but that was all.

I found a bucket under the sink, gave it to him and told him to go back into the classroom and that I would see him at the end of the day.

The receptionist asked, "Aren't you going to take him home?"

"No." I said, "I'm not going to teach my kid that if you feel sick, you go home. I'm going to teach my kid that if you feel sick, you grab a bucket and you crack on."

He was fine.

Anyway, I digress. My point is that a sick child at school is about the only emergency I've ever been called for and if I wasn't available, they'd have called my wife or a grandparent.

We give ourselves so much importance that we need to be contactable at all times.

You are not the president of America. It will be ok.

When I did the re-write of my previous book "Selling to Serve," I wrote 4,000 words a day for two weeks straight.

I ignored everyone and everything.

My wife was not happy with me, and I was ok with that.

I had to become focused and selfish, but for a good reason… I knew that accountants and bookkeepers desperately needed help with the way that they priced and sold their services.

Timewise, the world was in lockdown because of the pandemic, there was so much uncertainty and these firms needed help.

It became a No. 1 bestseller within its first week and is still the highest rated book in the world for practice management.

But if I'd have been overly concerned with getting the cold shoulder from my wife for a couple of weeks, it may never have got done.

When I recorded the audio version of the book, I did it in my garage on a very cold Sunday.

I'd committed to the editor that he would have the recordings first thing on the Monday.

I decided that I wasn't going to stop if I got tired, I was going to stop when it was done.

I was in there until 1am recording it.

I couldn't feel my feet they were so cold.

But in the moment, nothing else mattered and I did what I needed to do UNTIL it got there.

That is focus.

I was cold. I was tired. My wife wasn't talking to me. The voice in my head was trying to get me to stop

When you get close to achieving something, that is when you need to be most on your guard for Resistance showing up; the MOST focused, the MOST diligent, the MOST resourceful, the MOST relentless.

Many marathon runners quit at the 20th mile because that's when the pain is the greatest and the finish line isn't in sight.

They prepare for the 20th mile and so must you.

It's the 20th mile that requires your greatest will to overcome Resistance.

And it's at this point, when Resistance is throwing everything it has at you, that you must know WHY you're doing it.

Because only your WHY will drag you through, up or over.

"Smashing Into Resistance"

'So, after smashing into resistance yesterday I went out and smashed a renewal...$495 to $2,327 per month. I followed the process, shut up when I presented the fee, and client just said 'OK, I can't really do without you.'

Nickie Sheehan | Trio Accounting

PREPARE FOR OVERWHELM

I'm hoping that you feel suitably motivated and excited. You're starting to have a greater awareness of where you are now, you have a clear outcome of where you want to get to and by when, you know why you must get there, your mindset is beginning to galvanise, your mindstate is strong and you're about to be given the map.

BUT… I know what's coming.

Resistance is already getting ready to pounce again and after hitting you with a lack of time, it's going to hit you with overwhelm.

Overwhelm is a very debilitating state to be in and if left unchecked, can increase to stress and then depression.

Overwhelm is always a gift and it always has a very clear message attached to it, which I'll come onto, but it can be difficult to hear the message when the noise is so loud in your head.

Let's assume you're all revved up and everything I've said so far makes sense… what tends to happen next is the voice in your head pipes up and it sounds something like this…

Right… I've got to decide on what services I'm going to offer.

I need to make sure all my pricing is accurate.

What was that GoProposal thing James mentioned?

I might need to cross check the pricing with my friend who's also an accountant.

I need to update my engagement letter.

UNTAPPED by JAMES ASHFORD

Is my engagement letter even up to date?

Do all my clients need new engagement letters?

I've got to train my team on how to use it.

Oh shoot, Sophie's off next week so it will have to be the week after now.

I've got to split my clients into A, B and C.

I've got to decide which clients I'm going to start with.

I need to see what they're currently paying and how those fare to my new pricing.

I need to make sure I've got their phone numbers.

I need to setup my spreadsheet.

I've got to get someone to call them.

I need to schedule the appointment.

Should I use Calendly for that?

I've got to turn up to the meeting.

I need to produce the proposal.

I need to follow it up.

I can't do that until I've setup my services.

Do I need to setup all my services?

How should I price those services?

Am I doing advisory services now?

Did I say I need to make sure I've got their phone numbers?

Have I got their phone numbers?

Where do we store those numbers?

Should I setup a CRM now too?

Have I already got Calendly?

Should I train my team to do it?

Should I just do it?

How does GoProposal work again?

Will that sort out all my pricing and services for me?

Which client should I start with?

What's a C client again?

HAVE I got all their phone numbers?

Argggghhhhhhh… sod it… let me check my emails… I can solve that.

Can you see how quickly it becomes overwhelming?

It starts to build very quickly in our heads, and not only that, but we also start to do laps of the same tasks. So, what is perhaps 30 things to do, very quickly becomes 50 and because we don't even know where to start… We don't.

We distract ourselves with a short-term win of replying to an email, then making a cup of tea, then checking Facebook… instead of disciplining ourselves to do what needs to be done right now, telling ourselves that "I'm just not disciplined."

Abraham Lincoln said, "Discipline is choosing between what you want now and what you want most."

Jim Rohn said, "We must all suffer from one of two pains: the pain of discipline or the pain of regret."

So how do we solve this and avoid the regret?

STEP 1 – EMPTY YOUR HEAD

You can't have tasks doing laps in your head. Step one is to do a brain dump of everything you think you might need to do.

You can get your team involved in this too.

STEP 2 – CHALLENGE

Once you've got everything down, you need to challenge them.

You may have said… *I need to get all of my services in the system and priced correctly.*

I would say, do you really need ALL your services in there?

Do your C clients take all your services, or do they have a handful of core services?

We don't need to put a 3-year plan in place; we need a 3-month plan or a 30-day plan, so don't do more than you need to. I want shortcuts.

You may have said that you need to get your pricing perfected. Again, no you don't.

If you currently don't have a consistent pricing methodology, at best it's going to be 50% right. So, if you could get some pricing that's 80% right, then that's better than you have now.

Use a pricing methodology that's 80% right with the first ten, then 83% right with the next 10, then 86% right with the next 10 and so on.

Apple didn't wait until they got to version 15.3 of their iPhone software until they released it, they started at v1.0, then v1.1 and so on.

Remember, version one is better than version none, so just get started and we'll fix it as we go.

We're looking for progress, not perfection and the reason you struggle with that is because you're an accountant or a bookkeeper.

The very reason you came into this industry was because of a natural proclivity towards perfectionism, which is why, if I give you a set of accounts, you want everything reconciled to the exact penny right?

So that natural, innate tendency serves you well in your role, but not as a business owner or business leader.

The pursuit of perfectionism comes from an insecurity about being judged. We believe that if it's perfect, we can't be judged.

Again, that's great if HMRC or the IRS are judging you, we want a set of accounts or a tax return to be as perfect as possible.

But you have to take that hat off when you're working ON your business. If you want something to be great, you have to get comfortable with it passing through average, good and THEN great.

Your pricing doesn't have to be great for you to get started, but you have to start if you want it to become great.

Pricing is never solved, only ever tuned, so start and fix it as you go.

Challenge your list, cross out what's irrelevant and scale back those things which can be simplified.

STEP 3 – CHUNKING

The next step is to breakdown your individual tasks into chunks of activities. This process is called chunking.

For example, you could group all those activities into three chunks; three defined results, which could be…

1. GoProposal is setup to a point where we can use it with our clients to ensure a consistent pricing system, professional proposals and compliant engagement letters.
2. Appointments have been scheduled with the first 10 clients and are locked in the diary within the next 30 days.
3. Key members of the team have been trained in how to confidently and competently carry a fee review with even our most challenging clients.

If you want something to be great, you must get comfortable with it passing through average, good and THEN great.

We've been able to take what felt like 50 things in our head and got them down to 30 things. Then you got rid of the irrelevant ones and simplified others to get it down to 20.

Then we broke those 20 things down into 3 chunks: 3 key results.

All of a sudden, it's starting to feel much more manageable and all the time, we're reducing the chance that Resistance has to win.

How does that list of key results compare to the crazy internal chatter list from a few pages ago?

Can you see how it's possible to wrestle control of our mind?

KEY TASKS

Here is a list of key tasks that you may want to consider, that have been split into those three chunks. And below this list is a way of simplifying those tasks even further for you.

1. GoProposal is setup
    a. Define the core services we're looking to sell
    b. Get the pricing of those services to be 80% right
    c. Get the main engagement letter up to date
2. Key members of the team have been trained
    a. Run a series of test proposals
    b. Check the test proposals against existing client proposals
    c. Watch the re-enactment of a proposal meeting video

   d. Carry out a series of role plays with the team
3. Appointments have been scheduled
   a. Identify the clients we need to carry out fee reviews with
   b. Call the clients to schedule the appointments
   c. Have the fee review meetings
   d. Produce the proposals
   e. Get the proposals accepted
   f. Adjust their invoice and payment schedule to match

KEY TASKS MADE SIMPLE

I'm lazy. You should be too. I'm all for making life as simple as possible to reach my intended outcomes. Here's how you can take that above task list and make it super simple.

1. GoProposal is setup
   a. **Define the core services we're looking to sell** – This is done automatically when you sign up for GoProposal or can be imported if you're an existing GoProposal user
   b. **Get the pricing of those services to be 80% right** – Answer 3 simple questions about how you price 3 services for your most profitable client and the system will figure it out for you

   c. **Get the main engagement letter up to date** – If you're in the UK, subscribe to OverSuite within GoProposal and you will be given the most robust and comprehensive suite of Engagement Letters available on the market, that will be built for you within minutes
2. Key members of the team have been trained
   a. Run a series of test proposals - *Get your team to do it*
   b. Check the test proposals against existing client proposals - *Get your team to do it*
   c. Watch the re-enactment of a proposal meeting video – *watch it… with your team.*
   d. Carry out a series of role plays with the team - *Get your team to do it*
3. Appointments have been scheduled
   a. Identify the clients we need to carry out fee reviews with - *Get your team to do it*
   b. **Call the clients to schedule the appointments** – Outsource this to a specialist company. In the UK, we use MoneyPenny and Calendly to book meetings directly into yours and your team's diaries
   c. **Have the fee review meetings** – You take on the fee review meetings you want to do and get the team to do the rest
   d. **Produce the proposals** – GoProposal will do it for you instantly with no effort

e. **Get the proposals accepted** – This can be done during the meeting with GoProposal. If not, agree a follow-up date with the client, get it in the diary and get it over the line

f. Adjust their invoice and payment schedule to match – *Automatically done with GoProposal*

STEP BACK FOR A MOMENT

I'm trying to help you solve the fundamental challenge in your accounting business that is causing 99% of your problems.

Whilst this may seem like a daunting task, I'm helping you to break this down into three chunks and then into a series of critical tasks, which again, I'm trying to remove as much of the burden from you as possible.

Effectively, I'm helping you to remove as many obstacles as possible in order to make this breakthrough a reality.

You are literally 30 days from having a significant breakthrough in your business and I'm doing everything I can to make this as simple and as smooth as possible.

This IS happening… but only if you take MASSIVE action.

Taking notes; taking inspiration from what I'm sharing is nice, but it won't affect anything in a material way.

I want your life to change for the better.

I want you to have more money, more free time and more energy, but I can only take you so far.

YOU have to be the one to do this, but here's why it's hard…

As I said before, moving forward with this is like facing the wrong way on a downward escalator.

If you stand still… you go backwards and down.

If you walk… you stay still.

To move forwards and up requires massive action...You have to run, with every fibre of your being to fight against the Resistance.

You don't have to tackle the critical tasks in order.

The one task that deserves the most and immediate effort is to… **schedule the appointments.**

There is something about setting a date in the diary and making that commitment, that will force the other actions to happen.

There is nothing quite like a looming deadline to force you to do what you need to do.

Make the commitment to the outcome.

If you delay this action, you will allow space for Resistance to show up.

Speed will help you to beat Resistance.

BREAKTHROUGH ACTIVITY

1. You need to write down your WHY that will motivate you and drive you through the RESISTANCE you're going to face.
2. Put your OUTCOME and your WHY somewhere you will see it every day and commit to it like your life depends on it (because it does).
3. Establish the tasks that you think need to be done to achieve the outcome and chunk them into the KEY RESULTS you want to achieve.
4. Get yourself clear on WHY those Key Results are important to you.
5. Schedule, assign or outsource those tasks.
6. TAKE MASSIVE ACTION... TODAY.

"Find the force to take on the Resistance"

'So, one of my earliest clients when I first started in practice about 25 years ago, had a heating and plumbing business but their real passion was canal boats.

About eight years ago we helped them achieve their lifetime goal of setting up a chandlery, moorings facility for other canal boats, a small grocery and fuel filling station for boat owners on a canal way.

The clients are now in their 60's and are a lovely couple. However, I had not had a fee review since 2014 - because I liked them so much and they worked hard for everything.

Had a zoom meeting just now, had a quick review of how well the business was doing. Did a live GoProposal fee review, they appreciated the detail I went through with the pricing, and they accepted an increase of £120pm and they thanked me for all the help over the years and were happy to pay for the value they were getting.

Great way to end the week. Thanks, James, for giving me the confidence to find the force to take on the resistance!'

Bharat Hathi | BDH Chartered Certified Accountants

PART 6
THE WINNING PLAN

MAKING IT HAPPEN

Hopefully by this point you have a clear **outcome** you want to reach, you know **why** you need to get there, you have a **set of tasks** that take you to the point of sitting down face-to-face (or virtually) with a client, to review their service level and fees and you have already made some progress towards making that happen.

If you have, well done, we are about to move into exactly what happens during that service review and how to handle the question you're most afraid of.

If you haven't, why not? Seriously, why not?

What's stopping you?

What's holding you back?

What are you afraid of?

Who are you most afraid of failing in front of?

Challenge yourself. Uncover those blind spots and take action.

I also want to remind you not to confuse activity with progress; any idiot can be busy, but being busy doesn't necessarily pay bills.

We need to get focussed on outcomes and getting there in the most efficient way possible.

Before we get stuck into this, review your action list and ask yourself... If I was suddenly invited on a holiday of a lifetime at the end of this week, and I *still* had to achieve my outcome, which of these tasks could be deleted, delayed or delegated?

MAKE TIME

The only thing that's going to hold you up in achieving your outcomes is time.

I believe that there are few problems in your business, which, with 20 hours of focussed effort, you couldn't completely remove or at least diminish it to a point where it's no longer a problem.

If you woke up an hour earlier, ditched House of Cards or Schitt's Creek for a week and worked from 8pm-11pm, you could find that 20 hours and solve anything on your list.

Now that isn't sustainable for a long time and nor would it be something you'd want to keep doing, but if continually being paid too little and continually working too hard for clients is a real issue, why wouldn't you just find those 20 hours to batter it into submission?

20 hours will solve most things.

That's all that's standing between you and everything you want.

Find the time and if you can't find it, make it.

Make a way or make an excuse.

SCHEDULE THE MEETINGS

As I've said previously, we can't easily carry out proper service reviews without first scheduling the meeting with the client.

I have seen people do this as a blanket repricing exercise across their entire client base with one mass email. I am opposed to this method because I think it avoids a lot of the conversations that need to be had, misses huge opportunities, doesn't allow you or the team to grow as individuals, doesn't do anything to enhance the client relationship and prevents a detailed engagement letter from being produced.

So fundamentally, you must schedule the meetings, before you can *have* the meetings.

Here are a few tips for getting those locked in the diary...

TACK IT ONTO THE END OF AN ESSENTIAL MEETING

You will have regular quarterly or annual meetings with each client, whether that's an annual tax review, signing off annual accounts or a quarterly tax return. You can simply extend that meeting to include a service review. They have to turn up anyway, so pin them down on having a service review at the same time.

SEND OUT AUTOMATED EMAILS TO GET IT BOOKED IN

Automated email systems are cheap and easy to use. Some of them can even be goal orientated, so once a client completes a task, such as booking a meeting in your diary, the email sequence stops. It's very easy to use an automated system to send an email out encouraging them to book an appointment with you. If you would like an email script to copy and paste, please go to **goproposal.com/untapped** and grab that. You don't have to give us your details, just go and grab it.

"Use James' Email Script"

'Wanted to share this to encourage people to use James' email script. Just got this message from one of my rapidly growing clients that I requested a review meeting with. I used a lot of the script and tailored it a little to reflect my relationship with the client which took away a lot of my resistance. She replied with:

Yes I was actually wanting to get a chat with you because finances are getting my head in a spin these days so was going to look for maybe a bit more one on one advice from you!'

Gillian Caughey | Fearless Financials

USE CALENDLY TO SCHEDULE APPOINTMENTS

There are many automated appointment setting systems you can use to schedule meetings in yours and your team's diary, on days and times that you choose, when there is no other conflict or meeting clash. You can set boundless rules around that which makes life easy. Calendly links can be embedded in your automated emails

USE AN OUT-SOURCED CALL CENTRE

Finally, you can use an outbound call centre to schedule the appointments for you. These are specialists in getting people on the phone and politely getting the meeting in the diary. You really don't want to be wasting precious time and energy getting the meeting scheduled. You want to use all your energy on delivering a fantastic service review. Outsourced call centres like Moneypenny in the UK, can be great for this.

PICTURE THIS

Imagine this running in your business... you setup a service review cadence for each client, that coincides with another must-have meeting.

On the month before, they receive an automated email with a Calendly link to schedule an appointment, and further emails if they don't respond.

If they still don't book it, your outbound call centre calls and gets them in the diary for you.

Then as you approach each month, the service reviews have been automatically scheduled for you and your team focus on delivering them to the highest possible standards.

Does that sound like something you'd like to happen?

With some simple tech, a few phone calls and a proven email script, you can have this system up and running this week, and then it's solved forever.

Now all you have to do is master the service review meeting itself, and that's next.

Just say to yourself…

This isn't going to be a difficult conversation; it's going to be an improving conversation. It needs to happen, and it will improve my business and theirs. And while this may come as a surprise to the client and while parts of the conversation may be tricky, I am motivated and educated on how to navigate those aspects. Here I go.

I worked with a sports company once who were selling their services into schools. I asked them what their biggest challenge was, and they said, "Getting past the gatekeeper," who was the person who first answered the phone.

I asked, 'What chance do you have of success if you call them a "gatekeeper?"'

Gatekeeper made me picture some huge, armour-plated troll guarding the door with spears and swords. How do you think that affected their mindset before they even picked up the phone?

"Why don't we call them the "facilitator?" I asked.

Doesn't that just change your mindset immediately? And in turn it will change theirs too.

Arm yourself and get prepared, both in terms of physical assets and in your thinking.

2. POSITIVE INTENTIONS

Starting and ending the meeting with a positive intention is so powerful.

It means that regardless of what happens during the meeting, it starts positively and end positively.

It also communicates to the client exactly where this is going and why.

I used this technique for a number of years, but I really developed a deep understanding of this technique, from one of the world's leading hostage negotiators – Chris Voss.

In his fantastic book "Never Split the Difference," he talks about the importance of starting and ending meetings with a positive intention, so this is my take on that.

Once the pleasantries are out of the way and the meeting begins, I am going to open with a positive intention, which may be something like…

"We want to ensure we're providing you with the very highest level of service and to make sure that we're doing everything we can to support you in the growth of your business and improving your personal financial situation."

That is our genuine aim.

By starting with that, which is a very noble and worthwhile pursuit, it paves the way for us to talk about increasing fees, service level and additional services that fulfil that aim.

You need to create your own positive intention (or steal mine.) Whatever you choose to use, be very mindful of each and every word you use. Make sure there is no ambiguity or wiggle room and that there is strength in what you say.

3. FRAMING

The framing section of the meeting is designed to dig deeper into the client's challenges and needs, and its purpose is to frame up what you're going to offer them next.

This is why I'm not a fan of just sending out a blanket fee increase, because it avoids this key part of the discussion.

In the past I've spoken about the GLOSS Method® which is an advanced consultative sales technique and still very valid if you prefer to use that.

This is a simpler technique, because I'm focussing this book on speed of implementation and action.

There are 3 parts to the framing phase, with a recap at the end:

1. What's working well?
2. What frustrations do you have?
3. Is there anything more we can be doing for you?
4. Recap (Very Important) - "So what I've heard is..."

Let's break them down.

WHAT'S WORKING WELL?

This flies in the face of a lot of traditional sales training and techniques.

Traditional (and dare I say, outdated) sales techniques get you to start with, "Tell me what's going wrong." This method gets the client to focus on their pain so that ultimately you can swoop in at the end and be the hero with your solution. They even teach you to get the client to dwell on their pain and to dig deeper and deeper… "So, what problem does that cause?" and so on and so on.

And while we need to understand the frustrations they have, for you to ultimately solve them, you shouldn't start with it or dwell on it too much and here's why.

The number one reason a client *doesn't* say "yes" and sign up to everything you're offering, is because they don't want to make another mistake.

They've made mistakes in the past and they want to avoid making more in the future.

If you get them to dwell on their problems i.e., the mistakes they've made, you're reminding them of how lousy they are as a decision maker.

And then what are you going to do? Ask them to make another decision.

Do you think if they've just spent the last half hour pouring their heart to you about all their bad decisions, they'll be likely to want a make another one?

You've got to get them in a positive state of mind, and we do this by finding out what's working well and remind them of all the great decisions they've made up until that point, so they feel the most comfortable in making another great one.

Does that feel comfortable to you?

Just start the conversation with the open-ended question… "So, what's working well?"

As the client tells you, I encourage you to make notes with an old-fashioned pen and paper.

It not only helps you to process what's being said, but it shows the client respect and makes them feel significant, and that what they're saying is worth writing down.

I don't believe you can do this on a computer because it breaks the human connection, and they think you're really posting on Facebook.

A pen and paper are best for both of you.

WHAT FRUSTRATIONS DO YOU HAVE?

This is a fairly self-explanatory section. Just get them to be as open as they can.

It could be about the service you provide, their business, their team, their financial situation, their lack of time, their hobbies, their spouse, their kids, whatever.

Allow them to set what they're comfortable talking to you about.

Ultimately, you're trying to steer it back to how you can help them to overcome their frustrations, but for example, if they don't have time to pick their kids up from school and they want to, then you could look for ways to provide services that frees up their time.

Simply ask: "What frustrations do you have?"

IS THERE ANYTHING MORE WE CAN BE DOING FOR YOU?

This is a beautifully direct question.

This could be in the direction of improving the service levels they're *already* getting from you.

They may want to go from quarterly management accounts to monthly or they may want them one week after their month end versus three weeks.

Depending on what tools you use and how good you are at communicating what other services you provide, will determine how readily they want to explore the breadth of what else you offer.

They also may not know what they want and so you would have to be prepared to guide them, based on the frustrations they've already told you about.

Just avoid being in the painful position where you learn a client has gone elsewhere to receive a service that you could have provided, but which they didn't know you could. That one hurts.

RECAP (VERY IMPORTANT)

The final stage, once you've been through: 'What's working well?', 'What frustrations do you have?' And, 'Is there anything more we can be doing for you?' is to **recap.**

This is an especially important step in the process because it proves that you've been listening and it makes the client feel understood.

That's a subtle but significant difference. It's not that you *understand* what the client has told you, but that they **'feel understood.'**

This gives them confidence in you and what you're about to present next.

It's simply a case of going back through your notes on the three previous sections:

"So, what I've heard is...

You're really pleased with how your team is growing and that you're hitting all your revenue targets.

You're frustrated because you're still the bottle neck in certain processes which means you're having to work late and not get home on time.

And you think we can help you by taking over all the bookkeeping and providing you with a budget and a forecast for the year ahead.

Is that right?"

It doesn't have to be onerous.

You want the client to feel understood and you want to check what you heard is right and that you didn't miss anything.

5. REVIEW PROPOSAL

You now need to be in a position, DURING THE MEETING, to take them through the proposal, line by line.

This is key.

You can't send a proposal after the meeting because it's too much of a leap for the client to go from, revealing to you what's working well and their challenges, to getting a new proposal a few days later that's double what they're currently paying.

You need the ability to...

- Take them through this line by line
- Build up the proposal with them
- Get agreement at every step
- Present the fees

We want to bring the client on the journey with us and we want agreement every step of the way.

The way the conversation might go is...

Your revenue is now at £500k. Is that right?

We're still going to be providing you with Annual Accounts, yes?

You now have 7 members of staff on payroll, not 5, yes?

You now have around 50 transactions that need reconciling each month, which I can see here.

You would like us to do all your bookkeeping, which includes sending out invoices and chasing clients for late payments. Is that right?

You want your monthly management accounts preparing monthly and 7 days from month end, is that correct?

And you want a complete budget and forecast compiled for you?

Is there anything else you'd like to ask or talk about at this stage?

So, you are happy with everything we are going to be doing for you?

Great.

By the time you get to the end of that process, there is no confusion. There can be no misunderstanding. You've had agreement at every step of the way and at the end as well.

This should feel very much like a waiter or waitress reading back your order, to get confirmation.

Then, all that's left to do is to present their new monthly fee.

This is the moment you're dreading I know, because you're scared of what will follow, especially if there is a huge hike in fees.

But you need a system that enables you to present the fees clearly and transparently, there and then while you're with the client.

This should be being calculated in the background, while you're having your conversation, with whatever level of sophistication they require.

You also need the ability to break those fees down into very granular levels if needs be. You need the ability to present one overall fee, because that might be all that's required. But if not, you should be able to drill down into serve sections and specific services, if that's the level of transparency required by the client

Why do you need to present the fees while you're still with the client? Because you need to deal with their questions now, while you have their time and their focus.

And the way you learn to deal with those questions is going to change your life.

This is where you stand up for what you're worth and where you make a courageous step towards improving your life and the lives of everyone around you… I promise; it's that big.

You take them through the proposal, you get agreement at every step, you present the fees, and then you do the final thing.

And this final thing is critical to making it all work. So critical in fact, that this one point has its own page to make sure you don't miss it.

You take them through the proposal, you get agreement at every step, you present the fees, and then…

...SHUT THE HELL UP!!!

The customer may go quiet and if they do, that's fine.

They're just processing what you've shown them; they may need time to think.

My best advice, so that you don't ruin this step, is to sing a song in your head. Make sure it's one you know the full lyrics too.

Present the fees, shut the help up and sing a song in your head.

Let the client break the silence first and whatever they say, we will have a response for.

The beauty of using a system at this point to present the fees, is that it's not you saying what everything costs… it's the system saying it.

And then we move into handling questions.

Now think about this: you have to handle the questions anyway, so it might as well be now, while you have them. This is why you can't send a proposal after the fact, because you will create unnecessary friction and frustration.

Notice I'm not saying that we're going to be 'handling objections' here. These are just questions, and you **can** handle them.

And out of all the questions you could be asked, there's only one you're worried about, which is, "Why have my fees gone up?"

So let's focus on that one.

WHY HAVE MY FEES GONE UP?

There is only one answer to this question and it's short…

Q *Why have my fees gone up?*

A *It's a combination of factors, but mainly it's to enable us to keep giving you the high level of service that you want from us.*

That's the simple version. But there may be more that you'd like to elaborate on. It's more likely to go...

Q *Why have my fees gone up?*

A *It's a combination of factors, but mainly it's to enable us to keep giving you the high level of service that you want from us. Specifically...*

[and then choose the correct combination of these]

- ***We haven't reviewed your fees recently*** - This will be more regular moving forward.
- ***The service level has increased*** - give examples, such as more members of staff on payroll.
- ***You have additional services*** - explain which ones.
- ***Your revenue has increased*** - This means more emails, more queries, more phone calls and we don't want you hit with any surprise bills or feeling you can't call us.
- ***The complexity and regulatory requirements have increased, which means more work on our part and an increased risk*** - explain what.
- ***We have additional staff*** - explain benefits to them, such as faster turnarounds, quicker responses and a higher level of expertise.

- ***We'd priced some services to low*** - and we just can't keep delivering at that rate. We respect our relationship too much.
- ***Inflation*** - some services have increased in line with inflation.

Don't let inflation be the one you hide behind which can be what many firms do. It's like they're passing the blame.

Give the other reasons and own them. Stand by them.

When people ask you why their fees have gone up, it's not a criticism; it's a legitimate question and you need to have legitimate answers.

Now you've taken them through the proposal, you've had agreement at every step, you presented the fees, you shut the hell up, they asked you why their fees had gone up, you explained why, now what?

Well, there's likely to be one of four responses.

MOST LIKELY RESPONSES

That's fine [80%]

The most common response is, "That's fine."

They will just accept it and move on.

I appreciate that's far more boring than you expected.

All that stress and effort for that… that's fine!!! Really?!?!?

Yes, really.

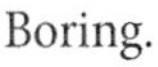

Boring.

NEXT!!!

I'd been waiting for you to do this and was surprised you hadn't done it sooner [4%]

The best response you'll get from about 4% of your clients is "I'd been waiting for you to do this and surprised you hadn't done it sooner."

4% is the 20% of the 20%. They're your top, most progressive clients.

When you get this one, you'll smile to yourself in disbelief because you never expected it.

I didn't really want to spend any more [15%]

The second most common response will be "I didn't really want to spend any more."

Don't stress this. How many times have you looked at something you wanted and thought that you didn't want to spend that much… and you bought it anyway?

This isn't an objection; it's just a whinge.

My initial response would be to be quiet, because they may very quickly transcend to ***"Actually… it's fine."***

Some proactive steps you can take is to…

A. **Remind them of the value** – Go back through the frustrations they told you and get them to conclude what's most important to them. It may go something like: *"Look, you said that you were spending Saturday mornings completing your bookkeeping and not spending time with the kids or playing golf. Is having your Saturday mornings back every week worth more to you than this fee increase?"* Put it back on them. Let them decide.

B. **Say:** *"If it needs to be lower, what would you like to downgrade or take out?"* Again, put it back on them. Let them make the call. Is having greater insight into their financials that important to them? Is having their monthly management accounts earlier important to them? They said it was, but now money's involved, so is it still?

They may need time to think. That's all fine. You just need to hold your nerve and stick to the plan.

Just remember, **never ever discount.**

If you need a reminder for how to respond to the "Can I have a discount?" question, scan here...

There's no way I'm paying any more **[1%]**

Now we're down to the 1%, and it probably won't be that many.

This is the one response you're most afraid of – "There's no way I'm paying any more."

In fact, it's probably safe to say that the entire reason you haven't increased your fees before now, is because of this very unlikely response to the question you've dreaded.

This one response has been blown up in your brain and kept you stuck for so long.

And the likelihood is that the people who would respond like this, are the biggest time wasting, energy zapping, pain in the ass clients, who don't value you, don't pay you enough, cost you money to serve and have crap businesses themselves. And these are the ones you're worried about losing?

They are the ones that are holding you back from having everything you've ever wanted.

But anyway, let's tackle the question.

If they say, "There's no way I'm paying any more." You have some responses which are…

- *I totally respect that. So, you can keep having what you're having, or you can keep paying what you're paying, but you can't have both. What do you want to do?*
- Ask what they'd like to downgrade/remove

- If you get to an impasse and they say they're leaving, explain you're sorry but you'll make it easy for them and offer recommendations for cheaper firms.

Stand your ground. Remind yourself why you're saying "no" to this client.

It's so that you can say "yes" to your other clients or "yes" to spending more time doing the things you love with the people you love.

But do you know what? Even many of these will come back round when they've calmed down and had a think about it.

Standing up for what you're worth is hard.

Not standing up for what you're worth is hard.

It's all hard.

Choose the hard that benefits you the most.

"He told me how happy he is with us"

'Moving on from the £11/month increase, today's renewal increase was £117/month for the same services, and he just said OK, approved immediately and then told me how happy he is with us and how much easier we make things for him (and we take the stress away) so double win. This was the one this month I was most worrying about too.'

Cheryl Sharp | Pink Pig Financials

6. AGREE THE OUTCOMES AND RESTATE POSITIVE INTENTIONS

At the end of this meeting, we want to agree the outcome.

Ideally, they're going to accept the new proposal during that meeting, either verbally or with a signature, depending on what is required.

If that's not achievable because they want time to think, then you need to commit to a follow-up date in the diary.

Ask them how long they need to make a decision and then agree the exact date and time you will be calling.

If they are a PITA client and they're being non-committal, then you may wish to take control of the situation and say, *"Look. If I haven't heard from you by this date, I'll assume it's a no and we'll send through our disengagement letter and cancel your payments. From that moment, we will no longer be responsible for doing any work for you and we will wish you all the best."*

Again, this is an extreme response so don't let it panic you, but at least you know it's there.

Whatever's happened during that meeting, we now need to end it with a positive intention as their final reminder of why we've had this discussion and why they're going to be paying you more money.

"So just to remind you, our goal is to ensure we're providing you with the very highest level of service and to make sure that we're doing everything we can to support you in the growth of your business and improving your personal financial situation. Thank you for allowing us to present a proposal that we feel will best help us achieve that."

And that is it. That's how we wrap up the service review meeting.

But unless they actually agree to this, nothing has changed. We must get them over the line.

CRIB SHEETS

To give you the best chance of doing this, I have created a form sheet to use in the meeting and a crib sheet to keep you in check.

They're on the following pages for you to go and steal or you can download from www.goproposal.com/untapped or by scanning the QR code:

Positive Intentions

We want to ensure we're providing you with the very highest level of service and to make sure that we're doing everything we can to support you in the growth of your business and improving your personal financial situation.

Framing

What's working well?

What frustrations do you have?

Is there anything more we can be doing for you?

Produce Proposal

- Get agreement at every step
- Present any new services
- Present the fees
- **Shut up**

Get it signed

- Handle questions
- Agree next actions
- **Re-State Positive Intention**

[CRIB SHEET]

Why have my fees gone up?

Just because they ask this, doesn't mean it's a problem. They just want to know. Respond with...

"It's a combination of factors, but mainly it's to enable us to keep giving you the high level of service that you want from us. But specifically..."

- **We haven't reviewed your fees recently** - this will be more regular moving forward
- **The service level has increased** - give examples
- **You have additional services** - explain which ones
- **Your revenue has increased** - more emails, more queries, no surprise bills
- **Complexity and regulatory requirements have increased** - explain what
- **We have additional staff** - explain benefits to them
- **We'd priced some services to low** - can't keep delivering at that rate & respect the relationship too much
- **Inflation** - some services have increased in line with inflation

The tricker responses

I didn't really want to spend any more

- Remind them of the value
- If it needs to be lower, ask what they'd like to downgrade/remove

There's no way I'm paying any more

- Totally respect that - So you can keep having what you're having, or you can keep paying what you're paying, but you can't have both.
- Ask what they'd like to downgrade/remove.
- If they say they're leaving, explain you're sorry but you'll make it easy for them and offer recommendations.

GO PROPOSAL by sage

"Love This Crib Sheet"

'After updating my prices and tidying my Line Items, I did my first Renewal today. I had prepped in advance a draft for £430 per month. They had a previous fee of £282. Anyway, they asked me to add an additional service which increased the price and took it up to £464. What an amazing start! I felt so elated when I came off the Zoom call as I felt it had gone really well, ticking all my boxes for getting agreement as I went - love this crib sheet.'

Jayne Smith | That's Ideal

GET THE CLIENT OVER THE LINE

It's your responsibility to take the client as far forward as you can during the meeting.

You have to present the services, the new fees, the proposal and the engagement letter during the meeting. This is imperative and certainly what the most successful and most profitable firms we're working with are doing.

A day later is 24 hours too late. Even 5 minutes after the meeting is 5 minutes too late.

They need to be armed with everything they need to pull the trigger during the meeting or none of what I'm sharing here will work as well as it could or should.

During the meeting, the client is now armed with everything they need to accept and formally agree to the proposal.

But… you can take them further.

Whether this is a face-to-face meeting or virtually, your client needs to have the proposal in their inbox.

- **Step 1** – Get them to find the email in their inbox. This ensures you've not sent it to the wrong address, or it's not gone into their spam folder.
- **Step 2** – Ask them to open the proposal on the screen, whether that's their laptop or phone.

- **Step 3** – Get them to go to the page where the acceptance button is.
- **Step 4** – Have this conversation:
    - **You**: *"When you feel confident about what we've agreed here and you feel ready to move forward, you just need to click this button to confirm. Is that ok?*
    - **Client:** *Yes.*
    - **You:** *Are you happy that you have everything you need to make a decision about this?"*
    - **Client:** *Yes, I am*
    - **You:** *Do you know when you're likely to make a decision about this?*
    - **Client:** [they give you a time]
    - **You:** *Great. Is that long enough? Will that give you enough time to think about it and speak to whoever you need to speak with, so you can make that decision comfortably and confidently?*
    - **Client:** *[They will either agree that time or push it out further to another time… let's say next Monday at 10am.]*
    - **You:** *Ok great. I'll put a note in my diary to look out for that coming through, and if I haven't heard anything from you by 12 noon, I'll give you a quick call, just to make sure I'm able to answer any questions you still have. Is that ok?*

You have now taken them as far as you can.

You have given them everything they need to digitally sign the proposal on screen and therefore confirm their acceptance.

If they haven't signed it during the meeting, we now know when they are going to sign it and they know we're going to be following up with them if they don't.

We're not being too forceful here. Instead, we're just being assertive and helping them to make the right decision that will benefit them in the long run.

But even having done all that, we still don't have to cross our fingers and hope for the best. There's still more we can do, because what we don't want is for them to now speak to someone else, who hasn't been privy to our conversations so far, and be talked out of it.

That person could wreck everything, so we need to keep them out, or better still, bring them in.

FOLLOW UP WITH A VIDEO

When the person has left the meeting, a huge gap forms for Resistance to show up.

This could be in the form of doubt, remorse for making the decision, their wife or their mate Geoff from down the pub.

I see so many people in our community say, "I've just sent out a massive proposal for double what they were paying before 🤞"

And it's that little 🤞 that always gets my attention.

I don't want you to rely on hope. I want you to rely on strategy and your newfound skills.

The moment the client leaves that meeting, you need to get in your car, follow them to their house, and be on hand to answer any question, they or anyone else has about that proposal, until they sign, even if this is a few days. Just camp outside their house.

I'm only joking, but that would work, wouldn't it?

What we need to do is the next best thing and send you, via video, so they can hit play whenever they need to.

Not only does this squeeze out Resistance but it adds a real level of wow to the situation, because you're demonstrating your expertise, your passion, your speed and your desire to provide an amazing experience.

People can't judge you by what you tell them, only what they experience.

The only reason they won't move forward with your proposal is because of a lack of certainty in either you, what you've suggested or themselves.

Sending this video of the proposal provides a great deal of certainty.

You literally open up the proposal on your screen and use a cloud-based screen capture software to record you, talking through the proposal and why you agreed on what you did.

It literally takes 10 minutes to do, you can include a small video of yourself in the corner to add that personal element, explaining why each service was included.

Depending on the software you use, you can even include the acceptance button in the video itself, which takes them straight through to the digital sign-off page.

You can then send that video via email, WhatsApp, and text if you want. Send it via multiple channels so they definitely have it.

I love using Loom for this, because it's easy to use, it's secure, its stores your videos in the cloud, you can embed the acceptance button in the video itself AND it tells you when they've watched it.

If you've never done this before and this an existing client who you've just hit with a higher fee proposal, it's going to show you in such a great light. Not only were you able to produce the proposal during the meeting, but within minutes of that meeting ending, they have a video of the proposal too.

What an incredible experience.

How do you think the client is feeling at this point?

If you would like to see one of these videos in action, go to www.goproposal.com/untapped and scroll down to **Follow-Up Video**.

If you watch the video to the end, I also show you how to embed the acceptance button.

WHAT IF THEY STILL DON'T RESPOND?

What if you've done all this, you've completed every step as I've described. You had a great state of mind, you produced the proposal during the meeting, you agreed a follow-up date, you sent the video, you tried following them up… but nothing.

They didn't answer. They haven't come back to you. They've ignored your calls. They've ignored your emails.

What went wrong? What does it mean?

NOTHING!!!

Nothing's gone wrong and it means nothing.

Life just happens.

People have partners and kids and work to do and parents and hobbies and shopping and staff and clients of their own and all sorts of stuff.

How many things are there that you've started the buying process for, that you really want, but which life has just gotten in the way of?

It's not that you don't want it, it's just not a priority right now.

So don't make an assumption.

Assumptions are likely killing your business in more ways than one (we'll deal with assumptions later).

You need to stay in contact with this person.

Explore different channels of communication and keep going.

WhatsApp voice messages, LinkedIn video messages, a card in the post. Just keep going.

APPLY HEALTHY PRESSURE

If all that fails, you can apply some healthy pressure, especially if they're a current client who you're providing services too.

You are in control of your business now, not your clients.

Depending on the client will determine your approach to the situation.

If it's a client who has notoriously being paying too little for too long and now you've presented them with a revised, higher fee and they're still not paying you, you can't let it drag on.

If you allow this to continue to happen, you're the problem, not them.

Explain that you're no longer able to work for them.

Ask them if they'd like to disengage.

Send them an email titled 'Would you prefer we disengaged?' or 'Sorry to see you go.'

Explain that you'll take their silence as a sign they'd like to be disengaged and then describe the next steps of that option.

If you've got it wrong and they would like to remain a client, then explain the date and time they need to sign it by in order to remain.

You can't let this drag on. Pick up the phone and call them straight away as well to explain the email you've just sent.

If this is a good client where you've added more additional services such as bookkeeping, because they wanted to get their Saturday mornings back, you need to send a different email.

"Do we need to revise your proposal?"

"Is the proposal I sent ridiculous?"

Explain the benefits of what was agreed and that if they want those services, then they're going to need to sign your new engagement letter and agree to the new fee structure.

If there are services that have increased in fees, you could also explain that if they don't want any disruption to their core services, then it also needs signing by a specific date.

One solid way to get it signed, is to have a new engagement letter. If it's a new engagement letter with changes to legislation and different terms designed to better protect them and you, then they have no choice. It needs signing by this date, or we can no longer act for you; it's out of our hands.

That would need to be made very clear in the proposal meeting

Regardless of what the client does or doesn't do, you have to take full ownership of this problem, otherwise it will always be out of your control.

You can't say...

"The client hasn't signed it yet.

The client is still paying their old fee, three months on.

The client won't get back to me.

I've tried leaving them a voicemail.

They don't want to pay monthly.

They're just refusing to pay any more.

They won't even have a renewal meeting with me."

All of that is blame and BS excuses.

There is only one truth that you can say…

"I have failed to get this client to pay more. I have failed to do this. Me. But…

…I will not allow this situation to continue any longer. I am going to send an ultimatum to them now. They either accept the new fee, sign the engagement letter and start paying monthly as of today, or they're gone as of tomorrow. I will not allow my team, my bank balance, my family and my sanity to suffer any longer as a result of me not taking full control of this client and my business. I am in control now and I am not going to let this continue for a moment longer. NEXT!!!"

Apply the right amount of pressure that is appropriate to that situation, but make it happen and if it doesn't, know that there is only you to blame.

If you make this mistake once, it's a lesson, but if you make it twice, it's a choice.

"Is the Proposal I Sent Ridiculous?"

'Here's the response to the "Is the proposal I sent ridiculous?" email I sent. Thank you, James,

Apologies for the slight radio silence on our end – been a hectic couple of weeks!

The proposal wasn't ridiculous at all. We do have a few queries/questions around some of the quoted fees, but it made sense overall.'

Susan Tinel | April 15 Taxes Inc.

I'm now confident that with what I've shared with you here and the additional resources I've directed you to, you have everything you need to know to make this happen.

But knowing is not enough, we must do.

So how do we go from *knowing* how to make it happen, to actually making it happen and what could prevent that?

MAKING THIS HAPPEN

It can be a big leap to go from reading something on paper to the rubber hitting the road.

You don't read how to drive a car and then start driving a car; there's a process and some steps you have to take first before you feel comfortable.

ROLE PLAY

You're going to need to role play, although I hate that phrase, because it either fills you with dread or fills you with too much excitement and neither are useful here.

We'll rename it Ninja Training, because it's very much like martial art training.

I'm a second dan black belt in Combat Ju-Jitsu.

Every week for years we would step onto the mat and train every type of attack, every defence, every scenario, with big people, small people, aggressive people, in the dark, wearing full work clothes, everything.

We would train hard so that an actual fight (should it ever happen) would be easy and touch wood, I've never had to put it to the test.

I want you to become a ninja so that whatever you face, you can easily deal with.

Just like in martial arts, there's only so many scenarios to play out, only so many attacks, only so many defences to those attacks.

Once you learn them and drill them, you're equipped to deal with most situations.

That's not to say something couldn't come from left field, out of the blue and catch you off guard. Of course it can.

But the harder you train this stuff, the easier it will be in reality, and eventually it will become second nature.

So, your ninja training assignment is to work with a team member or friend, get them to play the part of the business owner, describe the different scenarios and run through them.

Get them to make it difficult.

Get them to have a really long uncomfortable silence.

Get them to be super angry with the fee increase.

The harder you train for this, the easier it will be.

You can have some real fun with this.

BREAKTHROUGH ACTIVITY

Watch the mock up proposal meeting with alternative endings

Setup your ninja training session and do it.

P.S. I would love to see a photo or video of you doing this, so tag me in on socials.

SO YOU'RE READY… RIGHT?

You have just been given the blueprint to conduct high level service reviews, that have been proven to successfully increase the fees of existing clients with the least friction possible.

I have prepared your mind to believe this is possible and challenged your mindset.

You are onboard with what I have laid out, you are on the boat and have everything in your capabilities and power to reach your destination: your outcome.

But all too often, I see Resistance creeping back in, getting you to doubt yourself and encouraging you to wait.

Let's wait until next year.

Let's wait for a better climate.

Let's wait until I have a bigger team.

Let's wait until our service level is better.

Let's wait for more favourable winds.

But it has nothing to do with the direction of the winds, does it?

As John A. Shedd said… "While the safest place for a boat is in the harbour, that's not what boats are built for."

We must marshal our abilities, assemble our crew, galvanise our mind and do everything we can to venture out into unchartered territories, knowing that we have the map and the mindset to succeed.

The rest of this book is dedicated to making sure that there are no cracks in the boat and giving you the best send off into the sunset I can.

This will be the final shove you need to leave the safety of the harbour and to go in search of the treasure that awaits you.

"From a guy who thought he wasn't intelligent or confident enough…"

'Had to share this one as I'm both buzzing and a bit shell shocked. Just had a renewal confirmed for a whopping £2.7k +vat per month!!! Mind blown!

The client was paying around £260 per month and things have REALLY taken off these past 6 months. Initially worried about the lift in fees and whether it'd make me look stupid. But I managed to shake off the thought and focus on the BEST solution for the CLIENT, and what I would need to deliver it.

I don't care what anyone else would charge or why. It's about thinking with compassion and connecting a problem to a solution, then letting them know your price to make it work.

I offered them a new group structure to add a new Holding Co + Trading Co, a decent suite of support with room for growth as things progress and lowest end of the scale on bookkeeping for the New Cos.

What's crazy is the client was so happy to have the offer put to him, that he's shared our proposals/videos with a talent management company in

Oz (fairly popular outfit) that deals with clients in our niche, and they now want to send some UK clients my way.

Three have been sent across, I'd hazard a guess at about £1-3k per month each if I can get them over the line. And they fit perfectly in our niche!

So you may as well try to smash it out the park even if your inner chimp is telling you otherwise!

GoProposal is obviously a massive part of this and what has helped is laying out my service lines into departments (Your Finance Manager, Your Payroll Team etc). The client knows they can't get that mix of service & reassurance for under £40k per year through employees.

This is coming from a guy who thought he wasn't intelligent or confident enough to offer anything over £400 a month! Thank you once again!'

Max McHugh | Ocelot Accounting

PART 7
TIME TO ACCELERATE

KNOW WHO YOU'RE REALLY COMPETING WITH

After the second world war, Japan had been decimated and needed to rebuild and America had a duty of care to help them to do this.

Their infrastructure was heavily damaged, businesses destroyed, and in some areas, there was no water or electricity. They were literally starting from scratch.

The US sent over an engineer called Dr Edwards Deming who helped with the rebuild process and at the time, he introduced business leaders to a concept they called Kaizen.

Kaizen means continual improvement.

He got these business leaders to simply focus on being better this week than they were last week, even if it was by just a small step.

Deming knew the power of compounding and if you just keep making incremental improvements, the gains over time become enormous.

The likes of Toyota, Sony and Hitachi adopted this philosophy to rise from nothing to being global powerhouses… one small step at a time.

The reason most businesses don't achieve the level of success they should is because they either get to a point where they stop improving and become complacent, or they're continually looking for big wins that will leap them forward and don't believe in incremental improvements. This means that they're relying on getting a lucky break, but for the large part, remain stuck in the same place while they're looking for it.

In business, there's rarely one move you make, that causes the avalanche of cash.

It's just the slow, chipping away, day by day of making things slightly better, but to KEEP doing it, and never stop.

Achieving success is actually quite boring. It's just about making marginal gains, inch by inch in every area, week in, week out UNTIL you get there; and you WILL get there.

Constantly asking, how can this be better? How can we delight the client more? How can we have a greater impact on their business? How can we charge more for this service? How can we speed up this process and improve the accuracy? How can I remove myself from this process?

And it's not necessarily about winning, it's just about keeping playing as long as you can whilst getting better and better.

If that's your philosophy, I assure you, you WILL reach your goals.

You have to be relentless and patient.

We become despondent at times because it doesn't feel enough.

You look around at other firms on social media and you think you're behind.

It's easy to look at another firm and to compare yourself with them, but the reality is, you have no idea what is going on there. You have no idea how successful they really are, how impactful they are, how much money they're making, how much enjoyment they're having, how fulfilled they are, how much time they spend with their kids, how happy their marriage is, how much they drink, how much debt they're in. You don't know anything about them. So why are you comparing yourself to them and beating yourself up because you feel 'behind?'

There is only one firm you're ever competing with, and that's your firm last week, your firm last month, your firm last year.

You're the only business you really know and all we're ever doing is looking for progress, not perfection.

You don't have to be massively better. If you can make continual, incremental improvements, week in, week out, you win.

You will feel fulfilled, and you will outperform everyone else around you.

Don't compete, excel.

BE LIKE THE STARFISH, NOT THE SPIDER

There is a great book called the Starfish and the Spider, where the authors discuss the two types of organism.

Spiders have a central nervous system like us, where the controls for how that organism runs are in its head. Chop off the head or cut it in half and it dies.

Starfishes on the other hand have a radial nervous system, where the controls run throughout the entire organism. Chop a starfish in half and each half will grow a new half.

Most accounting businesses have a strong legacy of being spider organizations.

Information is pushed up through the various hierarchical levels to the people with 'the knowledge and the power' and decisions are pushed back down… eventually… maybe… but probably not.

This is a flawed model and we've seen large, long-established businesses and even entire industries get wiped out because of this thinking.

Starfish organisations on the other hand, educate and train their teams to build their knowledge and push the power to make decisions down, to the people with the information.

Pushing power down is far more effective than pushing information up.

It makes your company more agile and far less vulnerable.

That's not to say you don't want some decision-making capabilities or power to sit with the leadership team, just perhaps far less than you have now.

You can't grow your business, you can only grow your team and in turn, they will grow the business.

All you must do is to bring that team together and create the conditions for them to flourish.

Your team should have the tools and the knowledge for how to reprice a client.

Waitresses don't have to go back into the kitchen each time someone orders a meal, to consult with the chef over fees. They have the knowledge and the power to discuss dishes, provide a price, take the order and payment.

The chef would never have any time to cook.

If you're a partner led firm, does it really make sense for all repricing decisions to come back through the partner, when you have a team of people who are dealing with the client on a day-to-day basis, all of whom know the challenges and frustrations they face?

Why not give them the tools and training for them to do it themselves.

Of course, you can agree the initial service set and pricing parameters for them to use. That's the spider part that needs to be maintained. But after that, does it really make sense for the spider to stay in control or does that make your accounting business more vulnerable?

Does it make sense for the starfish to take over and to have an army of people driving your business forward rather than one or two?

Of the firms we work with through GoProposal, I can tell you one thing to be true… the firms who let a higher percentage of their team actively reprice clients within the system, make more money, have greater staff morale, have more impact on the clients and are better protected through constantly updated engagement letters.

And that makes perfect sense.

Imagine two firms, each with 20 staff and let's say two partners each.

In one firm, only the partners can reprice and *maybe* the office manager.

In the other firm, all 20 staff can confidently reprice clients and have the power to increase service levels and fees with whatever level of frequency they deem appropriate.

Which of them will grow, and grow in a more stable fashion?

Be more like a starfish and less like a spider.

MAKE THESE FOUR AGREEMENTS

There's a great book called "The Four Agreements" by Don Miguel Ruiz.

This book changed my life and I encourage all accounting businesses to adopt these four agreements because if you do, the majority of your problems, pain, drama and frustration will evaporate from your life.

The four agreements are…

- Be Impeccable with Your Word
- Don't Take Anything Personally
- Don't Make Assumptions
- Always Do Your Best

The book, although short, is very deep and very spiritual.

I am going to attempt to share my understanding of these agreements with you and apply them to your business interactions, but I highly recommend you get the book as Ruiz goes into great depth and explains them in profound ways that will change your life (bold claim I know).

BE IMPECCABLE WITH YOUR WORD

When I talk to accountants, bookkeepers and business owners in general, I'm always very interested in the words they say.

Words are hugely powerful. Words alone, have the power to start world wars, leading to destruction and the death of millions of people. They are that powerful, so never underestimate their impact in your business and your life.

The words we use, reflect the agreements we have with ourselves.

An agreement is a belief you have about yourself or your business or the world or what's possible, and you will always act in accordance with your beliefs.

Those agreements could have been formed long ago without our awareness or our consent, and unpicking them is a real challenge, because you first must have awareness that they're there.

A teacher telling you you're stupid.

A parent telling you you're not good enough.

A client telling you you're too expensive.

A member of staff telling you that farming clients are not prepared to pay any more than the low fee they've always paid.

The news telling you that the pandemic has had a devasting effect on all businesses and no one has any more money.

We hear these words and use them to form agreements with ourselves, often unknowingly, and then we communicate those agreements to others through the words *we* use.

I am *just* a bookkeeper.

We're *only* a small firm.

We could *never* charge any more.

That client will *never* pay more.

Now is *not the right time* to increase fees.

I'm *not sure* I can afford that.

Am I good enough?

Words.

Just words.

But can you see what affect they can be having on your life?

When I hear them, I become very interested because they give me clues to people's underlying beliefs and agreements.

I ask where they came from and ask why they believe them to be true.

Ruiz describes words as spells.

With just a few words, a spell can be cast over you that you carry with you for the rest of your life, and unless that spell is broken, you will remain in a state of pain and frustration. And that spell can be cast by others or even yourself.

But likewise, that same spell can be broken with just a few words, and then you're released to do great things.

I know at this point you are thinking, "Spells? What the hell is this guy talking about? I thought this was a book about increasing fees. This is too far."

Everything I'm sharing with you here has transformed my life.

I have gone from being in debt, marriage failing, business failed, blaming everyone, struggling with addiction and in pain, to building a hugely successful business, changing people's lives through the work we do, building a fantastic team, having a great marriage, being free from all vices and being financially free so that me and my family can live a wonderful life, without me ever having to work again should I choose to do that.

I have helped set countless accounting businesses on the same track and have witnessed in short time frames, marriages improving, stress decreasing, impact increasing, joy increasing, wealth increasing.

And all these transformations start with awareness of the concepts I'm sharing with you here and you developing new beliefs and forming new agreements with yourself about who you are and what's possible for you.

So believe me or don't.

Accept what I'm telling you about how words can cast spells over people for their entire life or can break spells and transform people's lives… or don't.

But I bear witness to everything I'm telling you in my own life and the lives of many other people I know and have personally helped.

I know the difference that can happen when someone goes from saying and believing, "I am just a bookkeeper", to saying, "I am a diligent bookkeeper, and I give my clients the data they need to make key decision about their business."

When someone goes from saying, "We're only a small firm," to, "We are an agile firm, full of enthusiasm and a desire to do the best for our clients."

When someone goes from saying, "That client will never pay more," and starts asking, "How could we get our clients to happily pay three times more?"

Can you see how with just a change of a few words, they start to change your thinking and your beliefs about who you are and what's possible? They engage your brain in very different ways. They give you a new focus which leads to different actions and therefore different results. And as those results start to appear, slowly, over time, those beliefs solidify, new agreements are formed

Somebody with a fearful, scarcity mindset says, "I'm not sure I can afford that." And their brain responds by saying, "OK." And that's the end of that.

Somebody with a courageous, abundant mindset says, "How can I afford that?" And brain responds by saying, "I don't know, but let's figure it out." And it goes to work doing just that.

They're just words. Yet they have the power to keep you completely stuck and in pain. Or they have the power to set you free.

People not only use words against themselves, but also against others. But know this, if you use words against others, they will eventually come back to hurt **you**. Let me give you an example of where this plays out throughout accountancy firms day in, day out.

You come off the phone with a client who's really pissed you off and you immediately start talking about them to other members of staff.

"I'm sick of that client. They're always late, they don't value us in any way, and she has no idea how to even run a business. And she wants me

to drop everything and do this work for her, well I'm not doing it. She does my head in."

Those words may have helped you to let off some steam, but you have now infected your team with your poisonous words and cast a spell over them.

Your team are now thinking in the same way and are focused on what you said.

You come in tomorrow and a member of your team says, "*Guess what? I've had another client on the phone today and they're exactly the same as the client you spoke to yesterday. I can't believe it. Why do we even bother? They're all bloody like it.*"

Then guess what? Slowly but surely, they do all become bloody like it and so you blame the clients.

You started it with your words; with gossip, because those words got you and your team to form a belief about your clients and to focus on only the problems and so that's all they started to see. And your business suffers as a result.

This is how words come back to hurt you when you use them about other people and especially when you gossip.

Gossip is one of the most destructive, corrosive things in your business.

If you have something to say about someone, say it to that person, not to others about that person.

Every word that comes out of your mouth or said quietly in your head is shaping your life in some way.

You have to be impeccable with your words, which literally means to use your words without sin; not to use your words against yourself or against others.

If you're unsure how you're using your words, simply ask yourself:

Am I speaking in terms of fear and hate?

Am I speaking with truth and kindness?

And don't confuse being kind with being nice.

Saying to a client, "*We need to double your fees with immediate effect, and I need you to start giving me your payroll data by 10am every Friday otherwise we will disengage you as a client,*" might not seem nice, but it is kind. Kind to you, kind to your staff, kind to the relationship and ultimately, kind to the client.

If it is truthful and kind, it doesn't also have to be "nice."

Say YES when you mean YES.

And more importantly, say NO when you mean NO.

DON'T TAKE ANYTHING PERSONALLY

When people say things to us, especially hurtful things, we take them very personally

How dare you charge me that much?

Are you trying to rip me off?

I can get this cheaper down the road.

You're too expensive.

You don't know what you're doing.

What do you know about running a business?

Just like *your* words are based on the beliefs and agreements you have with yourself; *their* words are a reflection of *them* and *their* beliefs and the agreements they've formed with themselves. They have nothing to do with you.

You only think they do because they've been directed at you.

If someone says, "What do you know about running a business?", what they really mean is, "What do I know about running a business?"

When someone says, "How dare you charge me that much?" what they're really saying is "Why daren't I charge more?"

Their words only have something to do with us if we agree with them because then, their words become our words and therefore their agreements will become our agreements.

Who am I to run a business? Why am I charging that much?

Someone's perception of you has nothing to do with you, but everything to do with them.

And to think it has something to do with you is actually selfish, because you believe it's all about you, when it isn't. You have put yourself at the centre of everything.

Ruiz goes so far as to say that if you take other people's words personally, it's the greatest expression of selfishness you can display.

There's a simple way to stop their words affecting you, which is to simply engage them in calm conversation and to seek the truth.

If someone says, "You're too expensive, you're ripping me off," rather than taking it personally and focusing on yourself, you could switch the focus onto them and try and help them. Try to understand what agreements they've formed with themselves that are holding them back.

You could respond with "Come on, why do you think that? What's really going on. Let me help. I'm on your side."

If you did this calmly, you might find out that they've been struggling to raise *their* fees. Maybe another supplier has ripped them off. Maybe his car engine's blown up and he needs to find the money. Maybe he's just not making money in his business. Maybe his costs are skyrocketing, and he doesn't know how to bring them down. Maybe material prices have increased, and he's scared to pass those costs onto his clients. Maybe his wife's just left him. Maybe his kid's ill.

There are a million things that could be going on in this guy's life, none of which has anything to do with you, but if you take his words personally, not only are you unable to help him, but you also cause a conflict.

You take it personally, you feel offended, so you feel the need to defend, and in that decision, you create an avoidable conflict, which you of course, blame the client for.

How much conflict do you currently have going on with your clients in either a small or large way?

And what if I were to say that you're responsible for it all, because if you hadn't taken their words personally, the conflict would have never happened and not only that, but you would also have discovered ways to help and serve your clients to even higher levels.

This requires great emotional intelligence. It requires you to remain in a positive, solid mindstate. It requires you to surround yourself with like-minded people and to guard yourself against any negativity entering your life.

This is not easy, but when you start to 'use your words impeccably' and you stop taking things personally, the majority of your challenges start to disappear. Combine them with the third agreement and they will, all but disappear completely.

Now occasionally, very occasionally, you will encounter a very destructive, combative, poisonous client. If you've done everything you can to get to the truth, to be kind and you've tried to help them and they're still like this, then in that scenario, they *are* to blame and need to go.

They are not a problem which can be solved, they just need to be removed from your life.

I've probably encountered eight people like this over the past ten years of dealing with thousands of people.

But I just want to give you a warning about these people here. If you ever encounter someone as poisonous as this, and you've been accepting their venom for so long, when you get rid of them the poison builds within them and they need an outlet. So, what they typically do, when they realise they can no longer control you, is attempt to control how other people see you, by poisoning them instead.

I've seen this very occasionally when a firm has a very bad client, they challenged them with a price increase, the client kicks off, they remove them and then they start bad-mouthing them on social media.

Just know this… it will pass. They will move on, and you will be far stronger on the other side. And I only warn you of this because if you sense this might be a possibility, this is where Resistance will step in and try to dissuade you from having the much-needed conversation.

You can't let it in, and you must be committed and firm in your belief that you are moving forward anyway.

The final thing to know about not taking things personally, is that if they tell us we're brilliant and they praise us, we can't take that personally either.

That, in some ways, can be an even more of a bitter pill to swallow.

We can't become addicted to their praise. We must be neutral if they are angry towards us or indeed if they praise of us.

I talk about this in depth in "Selling to Serve." We shouldn't be upset if a proposal is rejected or elated if it's accepted. A proposal being rejected creates space and time for us to do more with other clients. A proposal being accepted creates additional work and stress. Nothing is all good or all bad and we must be more neutral in our reaction to others, especially towards what they say to us.

DON'T MAKE ASSUMPTIONS

We've all heard the phrase, "When you assume, you make an ASS out of U and ME."

No, you don't. When you assume, you destroy everything.

As human beings, we have a deep desire to **know,** and we always have since the beginning of time.

And so, if we don't understand something, we fill that gap in our knowledge by making an assumption.

If you've chased a client 5 times after sending out a proposal and they haven't got back to you, it's easier to assume that they don't want to move forward with you or to think you're not worth it.

If a client says you're too expensive, you assume they can't afford to spend that much.

If we have a gap in our knowledge, we fill it with a story we assume to be true.

And when you make assumptions, take things personally and use words against yourself, you quickly slip into a rapid descent towards rock bottom, and you will abandon carrying out any more fee reviews.

Just picture it: You do three few reviews and you increase the first two, but then the third one gets a bit tricky.

The client tells you you're too expensive and you should be ashamed of charging this much, especially with everything going on in the world.

Now that's got nothing to do with you and everything to do with them and what's going on in *their* world. But you focus on those words. You drink their poison. You think it has something to do with you. You take it personally and feel offended.

You then talk about this client to other staff who say they've heard the same thing from other clients.

You assume you've got your pricing all wrong and you shouldn't be doing this, especially when we're on the tail end of a pandemic.

You use your words against yourself and convince yourself that you are in fact not good enough and need to raise the quality of what you do before you should charge any more.

You abandon all plans to change client fees for another year and assume that the problem will improve on its own.

But it doesn't, it gets worse.

You blame the client, you blame the pandemic, you blame this book, you blame me, you blame GoProposal, but is has nothing to do with any of that.

It all boiled down to a few words that you took personally, that caused you to make some assumptions, which formed new agreements with yourself, and you remained stuck.

As I planned this book, I really questioned whether I should include these sections because they go so deep. But to my mind, these are the real reasons why it never happens and unless we talk about them, nothing changes.

We have to delve into our psychology and try to get to the truth.

But we typically don't.

The reason we make assumptions in the first place is because we're afraid to discover the truth.

We lack the courage to ask the questions, that will uncover the facts; that's why we make assumptions and that's why we stay in pain.

When a client says we're too expensive, it's easier to assume it's because they can't afford us, rather than to find the courage to ask the question as to why they think we're expensive.

And we lack the courage because we're scared to death that the truth might be that we *are* not good enough and we *do* need to improve.

But if that is indeed the truth, then that could be the greatest gift to us and give us ways to improve.

The reason the waiter asks us, "Was everything was ok with your meal?" is because they don't want to learn the truth. And we know that, which is why we say, "Fine thank you." Even though it wasn't.

If they wanted to know the truth, they would ask, "How could your experience have been better today?"

We have to be courageous enough to ask the questions that will get to the truth so we understand what's really going on.

When a client says, "That's too expensive."

We have to find the courage to ask:

What have I not shown you about our service that would make you really understand the value and to see this as a fantastic investment?

Where have we fallen short historically in providing you with outstanding value and service?

What do I need to do, to give you total confidence that this is the right thing for you right now?

What would we have to do for you, for you to see this as the best decision for your business and for you to sign this right away?

Where else could you save money, so you could reinvest in the finance function of your business at the level we're talking about here?

Where are you really afraid of going wrong?

What would give you total certainty in this proposal?

These are courageous questions that are kind and just designed to discover the truth. That's it.

They're not used as some form of manipulative sales psychology.

They're just truth-seeking questions.

You assume your clients don't think you're good enough. You assume they can't afford you. And here's a big one... you assume they know what you do.

You assume that they know what goes into preparing a set of monthly management accounts or running payroll and then you're confused as to why they don't understand the value.

Your clients assume bookkeeping is straightforward and assume they can do it themselves. But what about when it goes wrong? Do they know what goes into unpicking three years of bookkeeping to correct bad practice and how much that would cost, or… do you assume they just know that?

Can you see how assumptions and lack of courage creates all of these problems; all of this unnecessary drama?

ALWAYS DO YOUR BEST

Throughout this book I have shared many concepts and challenged you.

Forget about how to carry out fee reviews. In the last three sections alone, I have challenged you to use your words impeccably, not to take things personally and not to make assumptions.

You just need to know that you are not going to get it all right and you certainly won't get it right straight away.

You just need to do your best.

Doing your best will make everything I've shared with you throughout this book, work.

That's all you can do… your best. And your best will change from day to day, moment to moment. Why? Because you're human. You're not a God. You're not a superhero. You're not a robot. You are a human.

You have flaws and vulnerabilities and cracks you're trying to heal and all of that is fine.

You're just trying to get a bit better, and you achieve that when you do your best.

If you attempt to do **more** than your best, you will exhaust yourself.

If you do **less** than your best, you will feel frustrated and guilty.

You just need to do your best.

That's all I need from you to make all this work. I just need you to do your best, whatever best looks like for you, today, in this moment.

Doing your best will give you the best chance of avoiding Resistance and mastering what I've shared.

And the only way any of us can master anything, is through repetition.

The way you mastered walking was getting up and falling over. Getting up and falling over. You did it a thousand times and you just kept going.

There was no point where someone said to you, "actually, stop this now, it's not working. Just sit on the floor all day."

No.

You kept getting up and trying again, UNTIL… you got there.

That's how you will master what I've shared throughout this book.

By trying and falling and then trying again.

When you first attempted to drive a car, you thought it was going to be easy because you'd seen many people drive you to different places.

It was only when you attempted to move the gear stick, press the pedals, turn the steering wheel, keep the car between the white lines, obey the traffic signs and avoid other drivers, that you realised how hard it was.

But through repetition you got there.

Now you drive to work without even thinking about it, whilst drinking a coffee, listening to the radio, chatting on the car speakerphone.

There is nothing you've ever mastered that *wasn't* because of repetition.

But when you start, you're not going to be a master straight away.

At first, you're going to be average, then ok, then good, then great and then… eventually… a master.

You don't have to be great before you start something, but you do have to start in order to become great.

You have to be comfortable with being average at first. It's just a phase to pass through, but you will get there.

We're not looking for perfection, we're just looking for progress, and always doing your best will ensure just that.

Take action, learn, make adjustments, repeat.

Ask yourself: Did I do my best?

You don't have to be great before you start something, but you do have to start in order to become great.

MEETING SCORECARD

In light of this, I've developed a scorecard to help remind you of these principles and score yourself against them after each meeting.

Dr. Edwards Deming said, "whatever you expect, you have to inspect." If you want your Service Review meetings to run a certain way, you have to check that they did, and you have to seek to continually improve them.

The scorecard can be used by you and your team to help you all with this. You can get a printable version from www.goproposal.com/untapped

My Name: Client: Date:

Pre-Meeting Positive Affirmations

- I am committed to doing my very best for my clients and my firm.
- This client is better off with me in their corner, doing all that I can.
- I know that words have the power to create or destroy.
- I will only speak with love and truth and kindness and not from a position of fear.
- I will have the courage to ask the questions to get to the truth.
- I am a good person.
- I am more than enough.
- Good things are supposed to happen to me.

Post-Meeting Scoring

	No				Yes
Did I speak with truth & kindness?	1	2	3	4	5
Did I say YES when I meant YES and NO when I meant NO?	1	2	3	4	5
Was I courageous in asking the difficult questions?	1	2	3	4	5
Did I avoid making assumptions about the client?	1	2	3	4	5
Did I help to remove any assumptions about what we do?	1	2	3	4	5
Did I start & end the meeting positively?	1	2	3	4	5
Did I stick to the structure of the meeting?	1	2	3	4	5
Did I end the meeting on time?	1	2	3	4	5
Did I get the outcome I wanted?	1	2	3	4	5
Did I do my best?	1	2	3	4	5

TOTAL /50

What will I do better next time?

GO IN SEARCH OF TREASURE

There's a story of a farmer from the mid 19th century.

He toiled the land on his family farm, as generations had done before him, but he always believed in more.

He had heard of people going off in search of great riches, so he sold the farm and went in search for his.

History is hazy as to exactly what happened to him and I don't want to add to that speculation, but safe to say, he didn't find any treasure and died poor.

The family who bought the farm continued to work the land as many farmers had previously.

One day a pipe got blocked on the farm and so the father asked his 15-year-old son, Erasmus, to go and find a stick to clear the pipe.

He went down to the riverbank to find a stick and while he was there, so the story goes, he saw something sparkling in the river.

He waded in a pulled out what looked like a rough lump of glass.

He showed it to his father and asked what it was, who explained it was nothing special, just some quartz or glass.

The boy played with it, with his brothers and sisters, for quite some time and eventually it found its way to the mantel piece where it remained.

A neighbour came round and spotting it, asked if she could look at it.

She asked the father if he knew what it was, and he said no.

She said, "I think it's a diamond."

To which the father laughed and replied, "Don't be silly, there's loads of them in the river."

She asked if she could send it to her friend back in Austria to see if they could confirm it.

A few weeks later it was returned with a note that said "Indeed, this is a diamond."

That diamond became known as the Eureka diamond, was over 20 carats in size, and revealed that their farm had been sitting on a diamond mine all along.

I often think of this story to remind myself that I am already sat on a mine of diamonds right now.

My staff are diamonds.

My clients are diamonds.

I'm a diamond.

I always believe that I already have everything I'm looking for, right here in my hands.

You already have enough, to achieve everything you're looking to achieve.

But here's the thing about diamonds that most people don't consider… diamonds don't look like diamonds.

As I said right at the start of this book: diamonds are rough lumps of rock, buried in the ground, covered in dirt, with sharp edges and the odd sparkly bit. They need to be knocked into shape and polished up before they start to resemble diamonds.

Most firms spend all of their time in search of diamonds, cursing their current clients because they don't look like what they believe diamonds to be.

Diamond clients don't look like diamond clients.

They're rough and need knocking into shape and polishing up.

You are sat on a diamond mine right now.

For my previous accountant, I was a rough lump of rock with sharp edges, spending £250 a month and unwilling to spend any more.

The next firm – MAP – polished me up and turned me into a diamond spending £750 a month, then £2k a month and then £5k a month.

I was the same lump of rock for both firms, the only difference being that one knew how to spot diamonds and had the ability to turn rough rocks into sparkly diamonds.

Now I'm not saying all clients are diamonds.

Some of them are rocks.

Some of them are great boulders, dragging you down and you need to get rid of them.

But I am saying than most of them are probably diamonds in some way, with the potential to be turned into far more valuable clients; more valuable for you and more valuable for themselves.

The healthiest position for you to adopt, that gives you the greatest chance of success, is to believe that you have everything you need right now; that you have enough; that you *are* enough.

I believe that the most successful accounting businesses in the world are not the ones who know how to find diamonds, but the ones who know how to create them.

You need to build a diamond generating machine.

THE REGRETS OF THE DYING

There are two driving forces in our life that are behind most of our decisions; they are the seeking of pleasure and the avoidance of pain.

Right at the start of this book I talked about how the avoidance of pain is the major driving factor in getting us to make key decisions.

I got you to consider some of the pains you wanted to avoid in three years' time, to help spur you into action, because sometimes the pain we're experiencing now isn't enough, but by projecting it into the future and continuing on that path, we get to a point in our mind in the future, that forces the correct action now, in order to set us on a different path to avoid that outcome.

That was why we did that exercise.

If the reality of your current situation isn't painful enough now, will it be if you continue on this path? Is the question I wanted you to consider.

We don't want to get to the end of the year and have regrets.

We don't want to get to the end of our working life and have regrets.

We don't want to get to the end of our actual life and have regrets.

Because you are going to die.

It's just a fact.

You are going to die.

Five of the most powerful words we can ever read.

We only get so many laps of the sun.

And when we get to those final days, we don't want any regrets.

So, what are the regrets you want to avoid?

I know what they are.

A great friend of mine, Paul Scanlon was a pastor of a very successful church in Bradford and then went on to work with leaders in businesses around the world.

In his role as a pastor, one of his duties would be to visit the dying and over the years he got to hear their stories… and their regrets.

And their regrets were all very similar, so much so that he compiled a list called the 5 regrets of the dying. They are…

1. I wish I'd worked less
2. I wish I'd stayed in touch with friends
3. I wish I'd allowed myself to be happier
4. I wish I'd had the courage to be me
5. I wish I'd gone for my dreams

Don't they make you stop and think?

And do you know how, with certainty, you will experience those regrets at the end of your days? It's whether you're experiencing them now and whether you experience them at the end of this month, at the end of this year.

Read through them. Are these not the things causing you your pain now?

Are these not everything I've been talking about avoiding throughout this book?

You thought it was just about charging your clients a bit more but no... it's about avoiding regrets at the end of your days.

And the way you avoid them, is by making directional shifts on the path you're on NOW.

And how do you do that? By following everything I've shared with you throughout this book...

Charge more

Have courageous conversations with your clients

Stand up for yourself and what you're worth

Focus on making more money so you can employ more people and free up your time

Use that time to spend doing the things you love with the people you love

Use your money to have a positive impact in the world; it will light you up more than anything you can buy for yourself.

Be happier

Aim higher.

Go for it.

Become all you can be.

Isn't that what I've been saying?

And if you were to do that, would that help you to avoid having those regrets?

This is why I'm so passionate about what I do.

It's why I say to my team… we're not selling software… we're changing people's lives… and I mean it.

And note this… it's doesn't say **I wish I'd achieved my dreams**. It just says **I wish I'd gone for them**.

Just to have stepped into the ring and at least took a swing for them is what life's all about.

What do you want? What do you really want? What's your dream?

Whatever that dream is, it's been given to you, and you can't expect anyone else to share that vision, it's yours.

I've already achieved many of my dreams so far in my life, but I was very careful who I shared them with.

The fastest way to kill a big dream is to share it with a small-minded person, and that may even be those around you; those you love.

Telling them allows Resistance to creep in.

Tell people when you're done, not when you're thinking about doing them.

BREAKTHROUGH ACTIVITY

1. What one, small decision could you make in your life today, to start reducing some of these regrets?
2. What large, tough decision would you need to make that would reduce or completely obliterate them?

FINAL THOUGHTS

If you truly believe in what I'm telling you here, if you work on yourself, if you uncouple yourself from fears, if you make all you can from everything you've got, if you overcome resistance, if you get your team involved, if you get behind this strategy, if you implement it, if you prioritise it and if you take massive action, you can grow your revenue from between 20% - 40%, by taking on no more clients and largely for the work you're already doing… FACT!

Just stop for a moment and think about what that would mean for you.

20% - 40% growth in your current revenue.

Earlier I shared a quote from an accounting business who have repriced 10% of their clients using these principles and grew their revenue by £36k. Multiply that out over the rest of their clients and you get to a £360k increase. That was from a £1million practice. That's a 36% increase in revenue, for the same number of clients and for primarily the same work.

I am working closely with a firm who generates £12m in revenue and over the next 12 months we have identified a minimum of £3.6m in growth from existing clients, that they're currently leaving on the table. That's over a 30% increase in revenue. The CEO said, "This cannot be achieved without the Untapped strategy and without GoProposal."

I talked about Kieran Phelan's firm which grew by 33% in 3 months.

This entire book was launched off the back of 100 small firms who collectively increased their revenue by over £1million in 30 days. If they continued that path, those 100 firms would have generated over

£12million in additional revenue from existing clients. That's incredible.

Since I did that project, I know for a fact some of those smaller firms have more than doubled their revenue from existing clients.

DOUBLED!!!

I have so many examples of these exponential growths in revenue that I have witnessed first-hand. And these are happening NOW as I write this book.

The pandemic was a huge storm shook the accounting industry up, but the dust hasn't settled yet. There are still turbulent times to come.

The pandemic forced governments to make severe economic decisions in a short time frame on an unprecedented scale. This highlighted their lack of insight into the real-time financial position of businesses and individuals, making many of their decisions unfounded, leaving them feeling very vulnerable.

It will take generations to pay off the debts that governments incurred because of some of those decisions.

Here in the UK, the initiatives around Making Tax Digital (MTD) for businesses and individuals will be happening soon.

This will enable the Government to be more than just, "one of the most digitally advanced tax administrations in the world," but also the enabler of small businesses and individuals to work smarter, identify opportunities for growth and be better informed of their taxes. This will naturally drive and boost the economy and hopefully recoup these debts.

This will be the biggest shake-up of the accounting industry we've seen in our lifetime.

It will force accounting businesses to develop very different relationships with their clients and for those businesses and individuals to operate in very different ways.

This will require large amounts of time, education, and focus.

Accounting businesses will need to become much more flexible in the way they charge fees, they will have to build in greater margins for the additional work and expectations, they will have to charge monthly, they will need to be able to update their engagement letters en masse and they will have to comfortably and confidently communicate these changes, the rising of fees and the heightened value they're now delivering to all their clients.

And when this all hits, if these firms haven't already sealed all of the leaks and already established a more profitable way of pricing their services and a firm wide strategy for maintaining high margins, they are going to hit this turbulence with alarming force.

The industry will certainly be shaken and while I can't speculate on what the effects of that will be, what I can do is help to prepare the firms who want to do good and who want to make a positive impact on the clients they serve, to be on the right side of all this when it happens.

I can't predict the future. But I can prepare you for it.

And I know that a firm that is highly profitable, with no leaks, solid margins and a strong team driving the strategy, will be far better prepared for the battles ahead, than one which isn't in this position.

At the end of the day, you are only competing with one firm… yours… last week, last month, last year.

You don't have to be great to make a start on this journey, but you do have to start to become great.

Start small, but start, and start now.

Please.

All I'm asking from you is your best, and your best will be different from day to day, moment to moment.

You are a great human being.

You are sat on a diamond mine.

You are a diamond yourself.

You are enough… you always have been.

You are capable of so many great things.

I know you're a good person.

I know how much you care.

You are deserving of so many great things to happen to you, but you have to believe that and then reach out and grab it.

It's far closer than you think

You will get there.

You just need to start… and then keep going.

Good luck my friend and keep me posted.

WHERE IS THE GIFT?

BURN THE BOATS

WORDS HAVE POWER TO CREATE OR DESTROY
BE IMPECCABLE WITH YOUR WORDS

NEVER GIVE IN
YOU'RE JUST 3FT FROM THE GOLD

NEVER MAKE ASSUMPTIONS

FIND THE COURAGE TO ASK THE DIFFICULT QUESTIONS

YOU CAN CHOOSE TO BE BITTER OR YOU CAN CHOOSE TO BE BETTER

DON'T TAKE ANYTHING PERSONALLY

YOU ARE SITTING ON A DIAMOND MINE
(And remember... diamonds don't look like diamonds)

GIVE THE PRICE
THEN SHUT THE HELL UP AND SING (IN YOUR HEAD)

ALWAYS DO YOUR BEST

YOU ARE A GOOD PERSON

GOOD THINGS ARE SUPPOSED TO HAPPEN TO YOU

YOU ARE ENOUGH

IF YOU CAN'T FIND A WAY, MAKE A WAY

START YOUR OWN BOOK CLUB

Organising a book club is a fantastic way to train your team and drive your accounting business forward. Just arm each of your team with a copy of Untapped and you all read a chapter per week.

At the end of each week, meet for half an hour and share your learnings.

When you've all finished the book, organise a longer session when you discuss key lightbulb moments, agree what changes you're going to make, create a plan and take action.

This is great for getting your team engaged and behind the strategy for driving growth and greater profitability in your business.

When you do this, please share photos, and tag me in on LinkedIn or Instagram so I can give you a shout out.

GoProposal is pricing, proposal and engagement letter software that enables accountants, bookkeepers & CPA's to price consistently, sell more confidently and minimise risk across their entire firm.

GoProposal will help you to…

- Remove the guesswork with a systemised approach to pricing
- Manage scope effectively
- Achieve and maintain high profit margins
- Remove yourself as the bottleneck and engage your entire team
- Carry out service reviews with ease, instantly, with a clear menu of services that you and the client can work through together
- Present the full value of your service in a professional proposal
- Generate fully compliant engagement letters that can be easily updated across your entire client base

You get a 30-day free trial. No card details are needed. Cancelling is pain-free. We will train you and your entire team to confidently increase your clients' fees in line with everything I have taught you here.

As a thank you for reading this book, I'm giving you 50% off a standard GoProposal plan with OverSuite included for TWO months. Simply sign up by scanning the QR code below.

If you're an existing GoProposal member and you're wanting to upgrade your plan to include more users , reach out to one of the Client Success Team and quote 'UNTAPPED' to get 50% off the upgrade for the first two months.

CASE STUDIES

"I now quote with confidence"

'This whole process has been a game changer for me - thank you. I thought I was pricing OK, but now I have the confidence to go higher. Three proposals done, two signed. I have a meeting setup today, which is a large catch-up job as well, so already GoProposal has paid for itself in full.

My mindset around being confident in what our business and my team is worth, has shifted and I now quote with confidence. I put down that I wanted an MMR increase of £300 - I have already smashed that. I still have some difficult conversations with some existing clients to have. But I'm feeling more confident thanks to this process.'

Kim Deere | Trekim Bookkeeping

"We just increased by ANOTHER £400"

'Had a call with a client this morning. We renewed 2 months ago and increased the monthly fee already by 50%. Just increased by another £400. Good start and client now paying £1000 a month. Didn't even say anything. Nice start to the day!'

Keith Lesser | Lesser & Co.

"I knew I needed to do this review"

'Another £800p/m increase in fees. I knew I needed to do this review, but I would have put it off for who knows how many months. I've also sent a £600pm increase to my biggest client. Thank you, James, for the push to do this. I would never have gotten round to doing it any time soon.'

Nicola Hageman | The Numbers Quarter

"Onwards and Upwards"

'Have started on reviews and some small wins but nevertheless a win is a win. One fee increased by £227pm, another by £223pm & a new client of £147pm with a catch-up fee of £875. These wouldn't have happened without this process! Onwards and upwards to the next few reviews today.'

Michelle Cowlin | Volarti

"That's 1/2 the new staff member covered"

'I have one more renewal to come in... and have gone over £1,000 per month increase. I can't believe it. That's 1/2 the new staff member covered.'

Carrie Stokes | Spotlight Accounting

"A fee increase from £120 to £278 per month"

'I've been a little bit quiet and wasn't feeling I was making much progress. However, I did a test run last night with a client (who is also a friend). Yes, it was awkward and will take time to master the art, but the result was a fee increase from £120 to £278 per month! Not a bad start.'

James Twigger | Accounting 4 Everything

"The wins are coming, I can feel them."

'I did my first live proposal yesterday and will hear back today. I would have normally priced it at £2000pa and the price came in circa £3800pa.

Can't believe I'm saying this, but I was shaking after the call as I was so nervous, but came off the call excited as I felt that the more times I can do this and refine what I'm saying and why, the better I will become. The wins are coming, I can feel them.'

Dipak Dhamecha | DD Accountants

"BOOOM"

'BOOOM. Had a client a few weeks ago saying they needed to take their services down from £300 a month to bring it in house as they need more in-depth info. Had a meeting with them Thursday and explained what I think they need from me and sent the proposal for £850 a month. He's just messaged to say he will be signing it today.'

Wesley Nunns | Nunns Accounting Services

"I stuck to my guns"

'Refused to do someone's payroll on the 1st. This new client has variable hours staff & wanted to pay them on the 1st, the previous accountant ran payroll on the 5th. He wanted to give me the hours at 8pm on the 30th.

I stuck to my guns and said I'm taking the day off tomorrow to wedding dress shop for my sister. I don't intend to work over the weekend. If you give me the hours tomorrow I will look at them on Tuesday. 3rd.

Another legacy client has delayed sending VAT info so will now be getting charged a late paperwork premium.

That's £360 of annual scope creep just from TWO WEEKS, stopped in its tracks. Is it any wonder we need to reprice? Imagine what 52 weeks of similar scope creep looks like? £9360! These small ripples are going places.'

Claire Davidson | Go! Accounting

READ SELLING TO SERVE

by James Ashford

You're not running an accountancy firm; you're running a business. But most accountants and bookkeepers don't have a business, they have chaos. You end up doing far more work than you get paid for and you're not valued enough by your clients.

Ultimately, you're not getting the rewards you deserve, which include financial rewards, the gift of time, growth, joy and fulfilment, which feels unfair and not why you started this.

You wanted to serve and impact your clients to the highest levels and get rewarded for it to. This book will take you on a journey that will challenge some of your most limiting beliefs, remove conflicting thoughts, reveal the blueprint for a successful sales system and give you the unshakeable confidence to do what you now perceive to be hard, to make life so much easier.

You will learn:

- The number one problem that's causing you to be overworked, underpaid, undervalued and how to fix it.
- Why you really think selling is bad and the two main reasons you continue to give services away for free.
- The reasons you still struggle to sell, despite everything you've read and been taught.
- Why clients really say "no" and it has nothing to do with a lack of money.
- The common objections to your services and how to overcome them, instantly.
- The step-by-step blueprint for the Effortless Sales System.

Get your copy now

Printed in Great Britain
by Amazon